SPIRITUALITIES OF SOCIAL ENGAGEMENT

Past Light on Present Life:
Theology, Ethics, and Spirituality

Roger Haight, SJ, Alfred Pach III,
and *Amanda Avila Kaminski,* series editors

These volumes are offered to the academic community of teachers and learners in the fields of Christian history, theology, ethics, and spirituality. They introduce classic texts by authors whose contributions have markedly affected the development of Christianity, especially in the West. The texts are accompanied by an introductory essay on context and key themes and followed by an interpretation that dialogically engages the original message with the issues of ethics, theology, and spirituality in the present.

Spiritualities of Social Engagement

WALTER RAUSCHENBUSCH AND DOROTHY DAY

EDITED AND WITH COMMENTARY BY
Roger Haight, SJ, Alfred Pach III,
and *Amanda Avila Kaminski*

FORDHAM UNIVERSITY PRESS   NEW YORK 2023

This series has been generously supported by a
theological education grant from the E. Rhodes
and Leona B. Carpenter Foundation.

Library of Congress Control Number: 2022923826

Printed in the United States of America

25 24 23   5 4 3 2 1

First edition

Contents

I – Introduction to the Authors and Texts   1

II – The Texts   21

Walter Rauschenbusch, On Social Sin
and Salvation   23
Selections from *A Theology for the Social Gospel*
  Chapter X: The Social Gospel
  and Personal Salvation   25
  Chapter XI: The Salvation
  of the Super-Personal Forces   37
  Chapter XII: The Church as the Social
  Factor of Salvation   44

Walter Rauschenbusch, On Prayer   55
Selections from *Prayers of the Social Awakening*
  Against War   57
  Against Alcoholism   59
  Against the Servants of Mammon   61
  Against Impurity   63
  For the Kingdom of God   65
  For Those Who Come After Us   67
  On the Harm We Have Done   69
  For the Prophets and Pioneers   71

Dorothy Day, On the Founding
  of the Catholic Worker   73
Selections from *The Long Loneliness:*
  The Autobiography of the Legendary
  Catholic Social Activist
  Paper, People and Work   75
  Labor   100

III – Socially Engaged Spirituality   121

FURTHER READING   139

ABOUT THE SERIES   141

ABOUT THE EDITORS   147

SPIRITUALITIES OF SOCIAL ENGAGEMENT

I

Introduction to the Authors and Texts

This volume highlights two writers who have left an indelible stamp of "social engagement" on Christian life in American churches. Their writings reflect a distinctive period in American history and an equally noted movement in Christian theology and spirituality. The timeline extends roughly from 1890 to 1941, when the United States entered into World War II. Walter Rauschenbusch became an increasingly commanding voice proclaiming the social gospel during the first thirty years of this timeframe. Dorothy Day entered into her lifework within the Catholic Worker movement, which she created with Peter Maurin in 1932 during the depths of the Depression. Rarely do people so different complement each other so tightly. Analogous times, immediate succession, a common faith, and passionate commitment to social justice bind them together.

A proper introduction to these authors deserves a full description of this dynamic period in American history. Expansion, development, progress, and creativity added up to pure social energy. Unchecked capitalism and exploitation of labor were an integral part of the push, and poverty and social degradation of workers were the byproducts. New York City, the hub of the eastern economy, exemplified the character of the age: urbanization, capitalism, industry, growth, progress, immigrants, and desperate destitution. It was the main port of entry for masses of immigrants who provided cheap labor. The counter ideas of socialism, organized labor, and class struggle motivated the left. Social Christianity, developed in England and Europe and addressed by Leo XIII in *Rerum Novarum* in 1891, where he advocated unionism, had also immigrated to the United States and was taking on indigenous forms.

The social gospel flourished during the first two decades of the twentieth century and beyond. It was followed by a new widespread and crushing poverty that accompanied the Depression years of the '30s. Everyone but a few suffered during these years. And then everything American was transformed by World War II.

This introduction to the texts on Christian social engagement approaches the two authors in chronological succession. In each case it first turns to the author and then to the texts and the ideas and values they hold up. The different genres of writing show different kinds of communication; Rauschenbusch's strength lay in social analysis and Day's in the narrative of her life's witness.

Walter Rauschenbusch

Rauschenbusch was born in Rochester, New York, in 1861. He was partly educated in Germany but completed his education at the University of Rochester and Rochester Theological Seminary in 1886. That same year he began work as pastor of a German Baptist congregation in a depressed area on the west side of New York City. "The church stood in a particularly depressing section of West 45th Street, near Tenth Avenue, surrounded by crowded tenements and noisy factories."[1] He worked there for eleven years, and the pastorate changed his life. He then took a position of professor of German at Rochester Theological Seminary in 1897 and taught church history there beginning in 1902.

His first major book, *Christianity and the Social Crisis*, appeared in 1907 while he was abroad on sabbatical. On his return the next year he found himself famous as one of the leaders of the social gospel movement. In 1912 he published *Christianizing the Social Order*, which had as its nucleus two sets of lectures that he gave in 1910 and 1911.

In April of 1917 Rauschenbusch gave the Taylor Lectures at Yale University, and these four lectures were developed further and published the same year as *A Theology for the Social Gospel*. This work is considered the classic statement of the theology underlying the social gospel movement. Early in 1918, Rauschenbusch became seriously ill, and he died of cancer in Rochester on July 25, 1918, at fifty-seven.

What follows brings a wide view of Rauschenbusch to a focus on texts chosen to represent his spirituality of engagement for social justice. It highlights his conversion during his years as a pastor, the character of the social gospel movement which he came to symbolize, the particular method of his theology, and finally the theological framework of his spirituality.

Ministry in New York. When Rauschenbusch assumed the pastorate in the working-class church in Hell's Kitchen,[2] he could not help but become deeply involved in the whole life of the people in his church. They were dealing with low wages, unemployment, subhuman living conditions, and political manipulation. He had not been prepared for that kind of assignment; his time was filled with immediate demands that seemed to distract him from what he had expected to deliver as a minister of the gospel. But he gradually assimilated; he underwent a gradual process of conversion to an interpretation of the gospel message of Jesus in terms of the "kingdom of God."[3] He later wrote autobiographically that his "desire was always for a faith that would cover my whole life. . . . And then the idea of the kingdom of God offered itself as the real solution for that problem. Here was a religious conception that embraced it all. Here was something so big that absolutely nothing that interested me was excluded from it."[4]

The social gospel movement. The phrase "the social gospel movement" refers less to an organized body of teaching than to a shared ideology within the churches of both the United States and Canada that responded to the injustices spawned by industrialization beginning in the second half of the nineteenth century. It had a deep background in nineteenth-century Anglican theology and in European social thought. It manifested itself mainly but not exclusively in the cities. The social gospel compared actual social life with the values of Christianity and reacted against the wholesale dehumanization of large sectors of the population. Positively, it generated many of the social agencies that have characterized American church life since then.

The social gospel predominantly thrived in Protestant churches, but analogous developments were seen in Catholic churches, bolstered by the encyclical *Rerum Novarum* (Leo XIII, 1891), which stimulated interest in labor unions. The movement did not begin as a theological school but had its roots in responses to the people in working-class congregations and their environment. But a theology was latent in the responses, and a large number of thinkers, both academic and pastoral, lay and clerical, began to formulate social, economic, ethical, pastoral, and theological analyses to accompany the spontaneous appeal to Christian values. "And even though the representatives of this theology of the social gospel were not all saying exactly the same thing, there are a number of axes of commonality which merit the generalized title."[5]

The theology for the social gospel. As background for the texts of Rauschenbusch, it is important to have an idea of the deep structure of the work—that is, the method that generates its insights and conclusions. This provides an answer to the question of where Rauschenbusch's ideas are coming from. A description of the method that produced the text offers insight into the way he thought. Descriptively, Rauschenbusch was a hermeneutical theologian. He offered an interpretation of the gospel of Jesus Christ in the context and terms of a social understanding of human beings, as distinct from an individualist conception of the human person. He read this anthropology of human solidarity as containing a social moral imperative in the face of widespread corporate suffering.[6] In plain language, the social gospel movement consisted of the Christian churches responding to the debasement of human life caused by urban industrialization, especially in the northern cities of America. In this context Rauschenbusch wrote, "We have a social gospel. We need a systematic theology large enough to match it and vital enough to back it."[7] This means that we have a living Christian social movement implying a Christian lifestyle and spirituality. In that light, he asked, what is the theology of the doctrines that justify or correspond with this spirituality? Rauschenbusch clearly illustrates how his experience was prior to his new theology. The spirituality he adopted in responding to the world around him provided the ground for theological interpretation of the traditional doctrines.

More pointedly, analysis yields the implicit theological logic that Rauschenbusch used to articulate his theology of the social gospel. One can read his mind as moving through three steps or components of a way of understanding. The first and most basic move lies in the responses of many churches to the social crisis. Together they formed a movement with leaders at all levels: pastors, members of congregations, and academics across disciplines, producing a substantial body of literature beginning in the last decades of the nineteenth century. For Rauschenbusch the intellectual movement was borne out in the politics of New York City.

The second step is a new appreciation of the social nature or character of human existence. This has a background in the nineteenth century with Marx, socialism, and the emergence of the discipline of sociology, especially Marx's implicit sociology of knowledge. These influences converge in philosophical and anthropological insights into the social nature of human existence: we are social beings and not an assembly of persons. Individuals always exist as individuals-in-society; human beings are socially constructed and interrelated. This means that one cannot understand human existence adequately through the human person alone: human existence is constituted in social solidarity.

The third step was the rediscovery of the concept of the kingdom of God in the gospels as the message of Jesus. For many theologians at the end of the nineteenth century, this concept correlated with this new sense of human solidarity. The kingdom of God gave the message of Jesus a seemingly direct relevance to the social situation of the present day.[8]

These three insights taken together gave birth to a method of theology that centers the message of the gospel around the kingdom of God as its center of gravity. This enables one to read that message as a response to the need for a theological interpretation of doctrine that explains and justifies the response of the churches to the social crisis. This method resolved Rauschenbusch's need to fit his education to his ministry and enabled him to understand the gospel and Christian doctrine in a way that responded to a lived problem of the time. The important terms that provide the continuity between the gospel of a past age and the present self-understanding of the interpreter are precisely a notion of social solidarity in the present. The kingdom of God that Jesus preached, Rauschenbusch concluded, addresses this human solidarity. Rauschenbusch uses these phrases to characterize his logic: "conceiving Christian doctrine in social terms" and "a social interpretation . . . of Christianity." In sum, the social gospel "fuses the Christian spirit and the social consciousness."[9]

With that formulation of the project in place, the development of *A Theology for the Social Gospel* follows a classical outline for representing Christian doctrines. He treats sin, the fall, the transmission of sin, salvation, the church, Christology, God, inspiration, prophecy, the Holy Spirit, sacraments, eschatology, and atonement. In each case he interprets the doctrines socially, in line with a social anthropology and in response to the social crisis. The texts chosen to represent Rauschenbusch's contribution to spirituality turn to the classical doctrines of sin and salvation to show how these doctrines entail ethical response and an engaged spirituality.

Social solidarity and theology, ethics, and spirituality. The readings deal with personal salvation, social salvation, and the role of the church as a medium of social salvation. They suppose that Christianity demands a Christian church and that the church mediates personal and social salvation and an ecclesial existence or way of life. In this way Rauschenbusch shows how theology includes both an implicit ethics and a set of values that define a spirituality. In short, active participation in the church, dealing with sin and salvation, involves a spirituality.

Sin is not merely personal; it is also social. Rauschenbusch deals with social salvation from social sin. The text presupposes the chapters that immediately precede it, which outline a social interpretation of sin. Sin cannot be reduced to personal sins or the sinful condition of the individual person. Sin also resides in groups and institutions, and they purvey it socially.[10] If salvation is salvation from social sin as well as personal sin, what will it look like? The texts discuss this question and lead to a constructive view of the Christian life.

Salvation is also social. Rauschenbusch shows that, when salvation is understood within the framework of the social gospel, the meaning of elementary theological terms shifts. "Thus the fundamental theological terms about the experiences of salvation get a new orientation, correction, and enrichment through the religious point of view contained in the social gospel."[11] This shift moves from a certain presumed individualism to a more solidaristic understanding. "Other things being equal, a solidaristic religious experience is more distinctively Christian than an individualistic religious experience."[12] The social gospel works on the basis of an appreciation of the degree to which social forces shape individual persons. The strategy of the social gospel is dedicated to the conversion and salvation of these super-personal forces of sin in society—that is, changes of social and cultural structures. The church thus appears as social grace. The most compelling idea of the chapter on the church says that, just as social organizations can carry the effects of evil and sin, so too the church can be an organization that bears salvation. This would apply analogously to other institutions as well. "A super-personal being [i.e., a social institution] organized around an evil principle and set on predatory aims is the most potent breeder of sin in individuals and in other communities. What, then, might a super-personal being do which would be organized around Jesus Christ as its impelling power? It would have for its sole or chief object to embody his spirit in its life and to carry him into human thought and the conduct of affairs."[13]

It follows that ecclesial existence can be regarded as a spirituality. Participation in the church implies that members behave according to the mission and goals of the church. Therefore, this construct of church as an organization responsive to social sin, and not just a collection of individuals seeking their personal salvation, implies foundational ethical values and a spiritual way of life. The common spirituality of ecclesial existence should operate in a way that resists the many constellations of social impulses that are objective, negative, injurious to the common weal and yet perhaps remain socially, culturally, and legally acceptable.

Prayer, therefore, should be socially conscious. Rauschenbusch's spirituality takes a more explicit form in the public prayers that he composed. They show the way Rauschenbusch's theology of social solidarity, within an ecclesial context of concern for social structures, expresses itself in prayer. His prayer describes social situations and represents them to God; he expresses powerlessness in the face of these conditions but asks for courage to address them with integrity. He prays as one standing before God as responsible, helpless, but willing to engage the social dilemmas of his time.

Dorothy Day

Dorothy Day was born in Brooklyn in 1897, the same year that Walter Rauschenbusch finished his pastorate in Manhattan and moved back to Rochester. For all his engaged experience, Rauschenbusch was an academic: historian, social analyst, church leader, and, finally, a theologian. He analyzed. By contrast, Dorothy Day also followed her father but into the world of journalism. She spent much of her conscious life writing or preparing to write in a narrative form. She bore witness. Both became iconic figures who in their personalities and writings exemplified a clear set of beliefs and values. But they did so in very different ways. Walter Rauschenbusch began his life with study in the seminary. Dorothy Day began her life as a seeker who, at the age of thirty-five, found what she was looking for: a cause and a way of pursuing it that would sustain her to her death. They both underwent conversions. Rauschenbusch discovered the rule of God and a whole new way of understanding his traditional Christian faith; Day followed a long journey of twists and turns until, in a very pointed moment in her history, everything suddenly fell into place.

The best introduction to Dorothy Day consists of her story. Given the range of her experiences in her early life, one cannot fully trust any selection of telling markers as explanatory. But three turning points in her formative years led chronologically to the creation of the Catholic Worker movement. The institutions which structured the movement were then so internalized that they came to define her identity.[14]

The university years. In 1904, when Dorothy was six going on seven, her father, John Day, moved the family to Oakland, California. He was a newspaper writer who had accepted a position with a San Francisco paper. They were there across the bay during the San Francisco earthquake of 1906. Right after it, they moved to Chicago, where he took another newspaper job. They first lived on the near South Side and then moved to the North Side. Dorothy continued her grammar and high school education in Chicago.

Dorothy had three brothers and a sister. She grew very close to her baby brother, who was born during her high school years. She was also active in her Episcopal church during this time. During her last semester in high school, she wrote a competitive exam for a scholarship and placed fifteenth among twenty winners. This enabled her to attend the University of Illinois at Urbana for two years. The year was 1914, and she was still sixteen.

These two years were marked by an experience of liberation and the formation of a new deep commitment that shaped the rest of her life. She did not have clear professional goals in her program. But she quickly became interested in social movements and the situation of the poor in American society. Relative to religion, she developed "a consciously critical attitude toward religious people who were so comfortably happy in the face of the injustices in the world." She felt "that religion was something that I must ruthlessly cut out of my life."[15] She joined the Socialist Party.

The birth of her daughter, Tamar. At the end of her sophomore year, Dorothy's father moved to New York, and she was drawn to be with her family back east. Although she thrived in the university setting, she wanted to work. She got a job as a reporter for *The Call*, a socialist daily, for a few months and then took a position with *The Masses*, a leftist magazine. In the spring of 1917 she was arrested for demonstrating for women's right to vote. She lived in Greenwich Village and became familiar with St. Joseph's Church on Sixth

Avenue. During one short period in 1918, she trained to be a practical nurse.

In the course of 1918–19 she met Lionel Moise, had an affair with him, became pregnant, and had an abortion in the wake of his abandoning her. On a rebound, she married Berkeley Tobey, a wealthy literary person living in the Village, in the spring of 1920. She was twenty-two when he took her to Europe, and they settled in London. During this time Day wrote an autobiographical novel entitled *The Eleventh Virgin*, which eventually was accepted by a Greenwich Village publisher. But the marriage with Tobey ended within a year, and in 1921 she moved from London to Chicago in pursuit of Moise. But she did not settle down there, and moved again with a friend during the winter of 1922–23 to New Orleans. While there, in the spring of 1923, her novel came out. Although the reviews were not ecstatic, she received a check for movie rights that temporarily lifted her from poverty.

Back in New York in 1924, she met Forster Batterham, a man from North Carolina working in New York; he became the love of her life for the next eight years. But he was hostile to the institution of marriage and organized religion and would not be moved. In that year she bought a fisherman's cottage fronting on the beach in Tottenville on the southern tip of Staten Island. She used it as her living quarters and a place to write. She shared it with Batterham when he was not working in the city.

The years 1925–26 deeply affected Dorothy Day. They were filled with happiness, probing thought, and frustration. Her belief in God began to deepen during this period. She became pregnant with Batterham's child in 1925, and Tamar was born the next year. On one side, Batterham refused to marry Day or recognize Day's new religious feelings. On the other side, she began to be attracted to and developed an interest in formal religion, practices of prayer, and official Catholic belief. She had, of course, the Christian training in the Episcopal Church during her childhood in Chicago, which she abandoned during her university years, but something new was going on here. In 1925 she began going to Sunday mass at St. Joseph's Church in Tottenville, evidently before she knew that she was pregnant. A year after she gave birth, in July 1927, Day had Tamar baptized.

During this year, Day was catechized in the Catholic Church by a nun in Staten Island, who prepped her in Catholic doctrine. The relationship with Batterham continued, and he remained completely inimical to her embrace of Catholicism. In December, after Christmas, she was baptized in the church in Tottenville, on Staten Island. During the next five years she lived in Staten Island and in New York, doing various things related to social justice and reporting on and participating in various agencies of social change.

Peter Maurin and the creation of the Catholic Worker movement. In December 1932, upon returning home to Manhattan from Washington, D.C., she found Peter Maurin waiting for her; he was a complete stranger. Maurin was a French peasant philosopher steeped in Christian history and a romantic utopian vision. His concern for poverty matched the depth of Day's. "There is no unemployment on the land," he used to say.[16] The initial encounter began a relationship that transformed her. It was Maurin "who inspired her to launch the *Catholic Worker* and whose ideas would dominate the rest of her life."[17]

The first copy of the newspaper *The Catholic Worker* was published on May 1, less than five months after meeting Peter Maurin. It was distributed in Union Square. She did much of the writing. The years that followed involved the moving of the paper's home, first to E. 15th Street. Day and Maurin gradually developed the houses of hospitality and the farms, while she continued to publish the paper. Other houses of hospitality sprang up in other cities. In 1936 Dorothy Day was in touch with thirty-three other Catholic Worker houses across the country. She did a lot of traveling to animate the houses and hold them together; she carried on an extraordinary correspondence; and she devotedly worked on the paper.

Institutional and personal spirituality. Dorothy Day's life was constantly changing as she tried to find her niche and raise Tamar at the same time. Everything changed with her meeting Peter Maurin. "At that point her life assumes a course of astonishing direction and consistency. Having found, through Peter Maurin, her essential program and spiritual compass, she steered a path that carried her for the next forty-seven years, one of the most tumultuous and dramatic periods in both American history and the life of the church."[18]

One way of analyzing the spirituality of Dorothy Day consists of looking at the basic institutions that made up the movement. She so thoroughly bought into Maurin's vision that it provided a skeleton for her activist spirituality. The movement consisted of three large institutions. The newspaper, which she named *The Catholic Worker*, was the first component. It provided a clear focus of attention. It reflected Day's desire to communicate, tell the message, and circulate ideas.

The houses of hospitality followed; they invited the poor and volunteer workers to live together in community. The houses themselves were poor and depended on gifts to survive and to offer hospitality, especially meals, to the poor. They responded directly to Jesus' revelation in Matthew 25: "'as you did it to one of the least of these my brethren, you did it to me'" (Mt 25:40). "He [Jesus] had set us an example and the poor and destitute were the ones we wished to reach."[19]

The third institutional leg was the farming communes. These were small farms where resident members, frequently families, ran farms for their own subsistence and to help feed the houses of hospitality.

The movement comprised other regular attendant activities. For example, the ministry of education, through informed but informal and free conversation, was a feature of the houses of hospitality. Both Maurin and Day were intellectuals; they engaged current affairs on a high level of critical perception.

But they shunned elitism and opened up reflection to the poor and those who joined them. Day personally and the houses of hospitality generally also had a strong formative influence on the streams of young volunteers who lived with or commuted regularly to form part of the family working for the poor. Another explicit concern of Day's was community. She wrote in the "Postscript" of *The Long Loneliness* that some say that the most significant thing about the Worker movement is poverty; others say it is community: no one should be alone. "But the final word is love."[20]

Day also wished that the Worker communities enter on spiritual retreat regularly. She invested time in finding the right people to offer such retreats in a way that could engage theological and spiritual matters that were relevant to Worker activities. She depicted theology as esoteric and claimed ignorance, but she did not hold it in disdain: "It seemed a wonderful thing to me that priests and laity could still become excited about points of doctrine."[21] Day's personal spirituality was schooled in traditional religious practices such as the rosary, but the Worker as an institution was not an official part of the church as a religious order would be. The movement and her spirituality were centered in the Catholic Church but had no other canonical bonds to the episcopacy than did the laity generally.

The Worker movement engaged Dorothy Day in an endless cycle of activity; the amount of time spent on any phase may have varied, but leadership demanded constant motion. It involved day-to-day dealing with the destitute who came to the hospitality house and "the poor, sick, and sometimes crazed individuals who made up the Catholic Worker family. It involved resolving conflicts and rivalries, assigning tasks, and overseeing the management of a newspaper along with multiple urban and rural households. It involved representing the movement through travel and speaking across the country, both to spread the message and to generate funds. It involved protests against war, racism, and injustice that occasionally landed her in jail."[22] It involved daily spiritual practices and constant letter writing. There were always letters to be written to everybody, and she never caught up.

Part of the attraction of Dorothy Day lies in the inability to place her squarely in a school or a larger social movement without remainder. Locating her and what she stands for in tandem with Walter Rauschenbusch complicates the taxonomy. She is American, Catholic, radical, servant of the poor, spiritual, and activist. She is absolutely unique and universally iconic at the same time: a strange mixture of pragmatism and romantic idealism. Throughout and into her old age she radiated transcendent Spirit.

Notes

1. Paul M. Minus, *Walter Rauschenbusch: American Reformer* (New York: Macmillan, 1988), 50. Rauschenbusch's congregation built a new church at 407 West 43rd St. and moved into it in 1890. See https://daytoninmanhattan.blogspot.com/2012/02 /1889-2nd-german-baptist-church-407-west.html.

2. Hell's Kitchen is the area west of 8th Avenue from 34th St. to 59th St. After the Civil War it became an area filled with tenement housing for immigrants, mostly Irish, but also the Germans in Rauschenbusch's Second German Baptist Church. The area was synonymous for crime, vice, poverty, gangs, and danger.

3. He had a lot of help from several quarters: the social commentary in the city, fellow ministers, and intellectuals like Richard Ely, who had studied economics in Germany, promoted Christian Socialism, and became a prominent leader in the social gospel movement. Rauschenbusch became a friend of Ely's while he was teaching at Johns Hopkins in Baltimore during Rauschenbusch's early years at Second Baptist. Minus describes these years of Rauschenbusch's pastorate in *Walter Rauschenbusch*, 49–70.

4. Walter Rauschenbusch, "The Kingdom of God," *Cleveland's Young Men* 27 (Jan 9, 1913), cited from Robert T. Handy, *The Social Gospel in America, 1870–1920* (New York: Oxford University Press, 1966), 266–67.

5. Roger Haight, "The Mission of the Church in the Theology of the Social Gospel," *Theological Studies* 49 (1988): 478.

6. The interpretation follows the work of Darlene Ann Peitz, *Solidarity as Hermeneutic: A Revisionist Reading of the Theology of Walter Rauschenbusch* (New York: Peter Lang, 1992).

7. Walter Rauschenbusch, *A Theology for the Social Gospel* (New York, Nashville: Abingdon Press, 1945), 1. Cited as TSG. As a historian, Rauschenbusch had written extensively about the history of Christian social engagement across the centuries prior to this essay in systematic theology.

8. Peitz analyzes Rauschenbusch's method in *Solidarity as Hermeneutic*, 75–104. Western theology later learned this hermeneutical method in formal terms when Bultmann used a Heideggerian framework to understand the gospel message existentially; Rudolf Bultmann, "Modern Biblical Interpretation and Existentialist Philosophy," in *Jesus Christ and Mythology* (New York: Charles Scribner's Sons, 1958), 45–59. Rauschenbusch interprets the New Testament in social anthropological terms. Dorothee Soelle will make this contrastive analogy explicit after Bultmann in explaining her political theology in *Political Theology* (Philadelphia: Fortress Press, 1974).

9. Rauschenbusch, TSG, 8, 3, and 20, successively.

10. This statement requires a subtle yet crucial insight into a distinction between an explicit, interior moral intention and a behavior that spontaneously acts out a pattern that is taken for granted. The distinction is well known today in the discussion of racism, where someone who is not consciously racist participates in cultural and societal patterns of actions that actually injure other groups of people. Analyses were graphically describing such patterns in the world of industry and commerce during this period. See, for example, Edward A. Ross, "Sinning by Syndicate," in *Sin and Society: An Analysis of Latter-Day Iniquity* (Boston: Houghton, Mifflin, 1907), 103–31.

11. Rauschenbusch, TSG, 105.

12. Ibid., 108.

13. Ibid., 119–20.

14. This chronology of Dorothy Day's early life is drawn from her autobiography, *The Long Loneliness* (New York: HarperOne, 1952); Jim Forest, *Love Is the Measure: A Biography of Dorothy*

Day, rev. ed. (Maryknoll, N.Y.: Orbis Books, 1994); John Loughery and Blythe Randolph, *Dorothy Day: Dissenting Voice of the American Century* (New York: Simon & Schuster, 2020).

15. Day, *The Long Loneliness*, 41, 43, respectively.

16. Ibid., 195.

17. Robert Ellsberg, *All the Way to Heaven: The Selected Letters of Dorothy Day,* ed. R. Ellsberg (New York: Image Books, 2010), 61.

18. Ibid., xxv.

19. Day, *The Long Loneliness*, 205.

20. Ibid., 285. Day has a section on community in the book. Robert Ellsberg thinks it defines the center of Day's inspiration. "But the major theme of her life was the search for community—whether in love and family, among friends and neighbors, in solidarity with all who struggle for a better world, or, on the supernatural plane, in the Mystical Body of Christ. Both in her youthful participation in the radical movement and later, as a Catholic, she resonated with the words of St. Paul: that we are all 'members of one another.'" Ellsberg, *All the Way to Heaven*, xxix.

21. Day, *The Long Loneliness*, 258. She was of course reflecting on Catholic theology before Vatican II.

22. Ellsberg, *All the Way to Heaven*, xxi.

II

The Texts

Walter Rauschenbusch, On Social Sin and Salvation

Selections from *A Theology for the Social Gospel*

From Chapter X

The Social Gospel and Personal Salvation

We take up now the doctrine of salvation. All that has been said about sin will have to be kept in mind in discussing salvation, for the conceptions of sin and salvation are always closely correlated in every theological or religious system.

The new thing in the social gospel is the clearness and insistence with which it sets forth the necessity and the possibility of redeeming the historical life of humanity from the social wrongs which now pervade it and which act as temptations and incitements to evil and as forces of resistance to the powers of redemption. Its chief interest is concentrated on those manifestations of sin and redemption which lie beyond the individual soul. If our exposition of the super-personal agents of sin and of the Kingdom of Evil is true, then evidently a salvation confined to the soul and its personal interests is an imperfect and only partly effective salvation.

Yet the salvation of the individual is, of course, an essential part of salvation. Every new being is a new problem of salvation. It is always a great and wonderful thing when a young spirit enters into voluntary obedience to God and feels the higher freedom with which Christ makes us free. It is one of the miracles of life. The burden of the individual is as heavy now as ever. The consciousness of wrongdoing, of imperfection, of a wasted life lies on many and they need forgiveness and strength for a new beginning. Modern pessimism drains the finer minds of their confidence in the world and the value of life itself. At present we gasp for air in a crushing and monstrous world. Any return of faith is an experience of salvation.

Therefore our discussion can not pass personal salvation by. We might possibly begin where the old gospel leaves off and ask our readers to take all the familiar experiences and truths of personal evangelism and religious nurture for granted in what follows. But our understanding of personal salvation itself is deeply affected by the new solidaristic comprehension furnished by the social gospel.

The social gospel furnishes new tests for religious experience. We are not disposed to accept the converted souls whom the individualistic evangelism supplies, without looking them over. Some who have been saved and perhaps reconsecrated a number of times are worth no more to the Kingdom of God than they were before. Some become worse through their revival experiences, more self-righteous, more opinionated, more steeped in unrealities and stupid over against the most important things, more devoted to emotions and unresponsive to real duties. We have the highest authority for the fact that men may grow worse by getting religion. Jesus says the Pharisees compassed sea and land to make a proselyte, and after they had him, he was twofold more a child of hell than his converters. To one whose memories run back twenty or thirty years, to Moody's time, the methods now used by some evangelists seem calculated to produce skin-deep changes. Things have simmered down to signing a card, shaking hands, or being introduced to the evangelist. We used to pass through some deep-soil ploughing by comparison. It is time to overhaul our understanding of the kind of change we hope to produce by personal conversion and regeneration. The social gospel furnishes some tests and standards.

When we undertook to define the nature of sin, we accepted the old definition, that sin is selfishness and rebellion against God, but we insisted on putting humanity into the picture. The definition of sin as selfishness gets its reality and nipping force only when we see humanity as a great solidarity and God indwelling in it. In the same way, the terms and definitions of salvation get more realistic significance and ethical reach when we see the internal crises of the individual in connection with the social forces that play upon him or go out from him. The form which the process of redemption takes in a given personality will be determined by the historical and social spiritual environment of the man. At any rate, any religious experience in which our fellow-men have no part or thought does not seem to be a distinctively Christian experience.

If sin is selfishness, salvation must be a change which turns a man from self to God and humanity. His sinfulness consisted in a selfish attitude, in which he was at the centre of the universe, and God and all his fellowmen were means to serve his pleasures, increase his wealth, and set off his egotisms. Complete salvation, therefore, would consist in an attitude of love in which he would freely co-ordinate his life with the life of his fellows in obedience to the loving impulses of the spirit of God, thus taking his part in a divine organism of mutual service. When a man is in a state of sin, he may be willing to harm the life and lower the self-respect of a woman for the sake of his desires; he may be willing to take some of the mental and spiritual values out of the life of a thousand families, and lower the human level of a whole mill-town in order to increase his own dividends or maintain his autocratic sense of power. If this man came under the influence of the mind of Christ, he would see men and women as children of God with divine worth and beauty, and this realization would cool his lust or covetousness. Living now in the consciousness of the pervading spiritual life of God, he would realize that all his gifts and resources are a loan of God for higher ends and would do his work with greater simplicity of mind and brotherliness.

Of course, in actual life there is no case of complete Christian transformation. It takes an awakened and regenerated mind a long time to find itself intellectually and discover what life henceforth is to mean to him, and his capacity for putting into practice what he knows he wants to do, will be something like the capacity of an untrained hand to express artistic imaginations. But in some germinal and rudimentary form salvation must turn us from a life centred on ourselves toward a life going out toward God and men. God is the all-embracing source and exponent of the common life and good of mankind. When we submit to God, we submit to the supremacy of the common good. Salvation is the voluntary socializing of the soul.

Conversion has usually been conceived as a break with our own sinful past. But in many cases it is also a break with the sinful past of a social group. Suppose a boy has been joining in cruel or lustful actions because his gang regards such things as fine and manly. If later he breaks with such actions, he will not only have to wrestle with his own habits, but with the social attractiveness and influence of his little humanity. If a working man becomes an abstainer, he will find out that intolerance is not confined to the good. In primitive Christianity baptism stood for a conscious break with pagan society. This gave it a powerful spiritual reaction. Conversion is most valuable if it throws a revealing light not only across our own past, but across the social life of which we are part, and makes our repentance a vicarious sorrow for all. The prophets felt so about the sins of their nation. Jesus felt so about Jerusalem, and Paul about unbelieving Israel.

We call our religious crisis "conversion" when we think of our own active break with old habits and associations and our turning to a new life. Paul introduced the forensic term "justification" into our religious vocabulary to express a changed legal status before God; his term "adoption" expresses the same change in terms derived from family life. We call the change "regeneration" when we think of it as an act of God within us, creating a new life.

The classical passage on regeneration (John 3) connects it with the Kingdom of God. Only an inward new birth will enable us to "see the Kingdom of God" and to "enter the Kingdom of God." The larger vision and the larger contact both require a new development of our spirit. In our unregenerate condition the consciousness of God is weak, occasional, and suppressed. The more Jesus Christ becomes dominant in us, the more does the light and life of God shine steadily in us and create a religious personality which we did not have. Life is lived under a new synthesis.

It is strange and interesting that regeneration is thus connected with the Kingdom of God in John 3. The term has otherwise completely dropped out of the terminology of the Fourth Gospel. If we have here a verbatim memory of a saying of Jesus, the survival would indicate how closely the idea of personal regeneration was originally bound up with the Kingdom of hope. When John the Baptist first called men to conversion and a change of mind, all his motives and appeals were taken from the outlook toward the Kingdom. Evidently the entire meaning of "conversion" and "regeneration" was subtly changed when the conception of the Kingdom disappeared from Christian thought. The change in ourselves was now no longer connected with a great divine change in humanity, for which we must prepare and get fit. If we are converted, what are we converted to? If we are regenerated, does the scope of so divine a transformation end in our "going to heaven"? The nexus between our religious experience and humanity seems gone when the Kingdom of God is not present in the idea of regeneration.

Through the experience and influence of Paul the word "faith" has gained a central place in the terminology of salvation. Its meaning fluctuates according to the dominant conception of religion. With Paul it was a comprehensive mystical symbol covering his whole inner experience of salvation and emancipation, which flooded his soul with joy and power. On the other hand, wherever doctrine becomes rigid and is the preeminent thing in religion, "faith" means submission of the mind to the affirmations of dogma and theology and, in particular, acceptance of the plan of salvation and trust in the vicarious atonement of Christ. Where the idea of the Church dominates religion, "faith" means mainly submission to the teaching and guidance of the Church. In popular religion it may shrivel up to something so small as putting a finger on a Scripture text and "claiming the promise."

In primitive Christianity the forward look of expectancy was characteristic of religion. The glory of the coming dawn was on the Eastern clouds. This influenced the conception of "faith." It was akin to hope, the forward gaze of the pioneers. The historical illustrations of faith in Hebrews 6 show faith launching life toward the unseen future.

This is the aspect of faith which is emphasized by the social gospel. It is not so much the endorsement of ideas formulated in the past, as expectancy and confidence in the coming salvation of God. In this respect the forward look of primitive Christianity is resumed. Faith once more means prophetic vision. It is faith to assume that this is a good world and that life is worth living. It is faith to assert the feasibility of a fairly righteous and fraternal social order. In the midst of a despotic and predatory industrial life, it is faith to stake our business future on the proposition that fairness, kindness, and fraternity will work. When war inflames a nation, it is faith to believe that a peaceable disposition is a workable international policy. Amidst the disunion of Christendom, it is faith to look for unity and to express unity in action. It is faith to see God at work in the world and to claim a share in his job. Faith is an energetic act of the will, affirming our fellowship with God and man, declaring our solidarity with the Kingdom of God, and repudiating selfish isolation.

*   *   *   *

"Sanctification," according to almost any definition, is the continuation of that process of spiritual education and transformation by which a human personality becomes a willing organ of the spirit of Christ. Those who believe in the social gospel can share in any methods for the cultivation of the spiritual life if only they have an ethical outcome. The social gospel takes up the message of the Hebrew prophets: that ritual and emotional religion is harmful unless it results in righteousness. Sanctification is through increased fellowship with God and man. But fellowship is impossible without an exchange of service. Here we come back to our previous proposition that the Kingdom of God is the commonwealth of cooperative service and that the most common form of sinful selfishness is the effort to escape from labor. Sanctification, therefore, cannot be attained in an unproductive life, unless it is unproductive through necessity. In the long run the only true way to gain moral insight, self-discipline, humility, love, and a consciousness of coherence and dependence is to take our place among those who serve one another by useful labor. Parasitism blinds; work reveals.

*   *   *   *

The fact that the social gospel is a distinct type of religious experience is proved by comparing it with mysticism. In most other types of Christianity, the mystic experience is rated as the highest form of sanctification. In Catholicism the monastic life is the way of perfection and mystic rapture is the highest attainment and reward of monastic contemplation and service. In Protestantism, which has no monastic leisure for mystic exercises, mysticism is of a homelier type, but in almost every group of believers there are some individuals who profess to have attained a higher stage of sanctification through "a second blessing," "the higher life," "complete sanctification," "perfect love," Christian science, or Theosophy. The literature and organizations ministering to this mystical life go on the assumption that it far transcends the ordinary way in spiritual blessings and sanctifying power.

Mysticism is a steep short-cut to communion with God. There is no doubt that under favorable conditions it has produced beautiful results of unselfishness, humility, and undauntable courage. Its danger is that it isolates. In energetic mysticism the soul concentrates on God, shuts out the world, and is conscious only of God and itself. In its highest form, even the consciousness of self is swallowed up in the all-filling possession of God. No wonder it is absorbing and wonderful. But we have to turn our back on the world to attain this experience, and when we have attained it, it makes us indifferent to the world. What does Time matter when we can live in Eternity? What gift can this world offer us after we have entered into the luminous presence of God?

The mystic way to holiness is not through humanity but above it. We can not set aside the fundamental law of God that way. He made us for one another, and our highest perfection comes not by isolation but by love. The way of holiness through human fellowship and service is slower and lowlier, but its results are more essentially Christian. Paul dealt with the mystic phenomena of religion when he dealt with the charismata of primitive Christianity, especially with glossolalia (I Cor. 12–14). It is a striking fact that he ranks the spiritual gifts not according to their mystic rapture but according to their rational control and their power of serving others. His great chapter on love dominates the whole discussion and is offered as a counter-poise and antidote to the dangers of mysticism.[1]

Mysticism is not the maturest form of sanctification. As Professor Royce well says, "It is the always young, it is the childlike, it is the essentially immature aspect of the deeper religious life. Its ardor, its pathos, its illusions, and its genuine illuminations have all the characters of youth about them, characters beautiful, but capricious."[2] There is even a question whether mysticism proper, with rapture and absorption, is Christian in its antecedents or Platonic.

I believe in prayer and meditation in the presence of God; in the conscious purging of the soul from fear, love of gain, and selfish ambition, through realizing God; in bringing the intellect into alignment with the mind of Christ; and in reaffirming the allegiance of the will to the Kingdom of God. When a man goes up against hard work, conflict, loneliness, and the cross, it is his right to lean back on the Eternal and to draw from the silent reservoirs. But what we get thus is for use. Personal sanctification must serve the Kingdom of God. Any mystic experience which makes our fellow-men less real and our daily labour less noble is dangerous religion. A religious experience is not Christian unless it binds us closer to men and commits us more deeply to the Kingdom of God.

Thus the fundamental theological terms about the experiences of salvation get a new orientation, correction, and enrichment through the religious point of view contained in the social gospel. These changes would effect an approximation to the spirit and outlook of primitive Christianity, going back [before] Catholicism and Protestantism alike.

The definitions we have attempted are not merely academic and hypothetical exercises. Religion is actually being experienced in such ways.

In the Bible we have several accounts of religious experiences which were fundamental in the life of its greatest characters. A few are told in their own striking phrases. Others are described by later writers, and in that case indicate what popular opinion expected such men to experience. Now, none of these experiences, so far as I see, are of that solitary type in which a soul struggles for its own salvation in order to escape the penalties of sin or to attain perfection and peace for itself. All were experienced with a conscious outlook toward humanity. When Moses saw the glory of God in the flaming bush and learned the ineffable name of the Eternal, it was not the salvation of Moses which was in question but the salvation of his people from the bondage of Egypt. When young Samuel first heard the call of the Voice in the darkness, it spoke to him of priestly extortion and the troubled future of his people. When Isaiah saw the glory of the Lord above the Cherubim, he realized by contrast that he was a man of unclean lips, but also that he dwelt among a people of unclean lips. His cleansing and the dedication which followed were his preparation for taking hold of the social situation of his nation. In Jeremiah we are supposed to have the attainment of the religion of the individual, but even his intimate experiences were all in full view of the fate of his nation. Paul's experience at Damascus was the culmination of his personal struggle and his emergence into spiritual freedom. But his crisis got its intensity from its social background. He was deciding, so far as he was concerned, between the old narrow nationalistic religion of conservative Judaism and a wider destiny for his people, between the validity of the Law and spiritual liberty, between the exclusive claims of Israel on the Messianic hope and a world-wide participation in the historical prerogatives of the first-born people. The issues for which his later life stood were condensed in the days at Damascus, as we can see from his own recital in Galatians 1, and these religious issues were the fundamental social questions for his nation at that time.

We cannot afford to rate this group of religious experiences at a low value. As with us all, the theology of the prophets was based on their personal experiences. Out of them grew their ethical monotheism and their God-consciousness. This was the highest element in the spiritual heritage of his people which came to Jesus. He reinterpreted and perfected it in his personality, and in that form it has remained the highest factor among the various historical strains combined in our religion.

These prophetic experiences were not superficial. There was soul-shaking emotion, a deep sense of sin, faith in God, longing for him, self-surrender, enduement with spiritual power. Yet they were not ascetic, not individualistic, not directed toward a future life. They were social, political, solidaristic.

The religious experiences evoked by the social gospel belong to the same type, though deeply modified, of course, by the profound differences between their age and ours. What the wars and oppressions of Israel and Judah meant to them, the wars and exploitations of modern civilization mean to us. In these things God speaks to our souls. When we face these questions we meet God. An increasing number of young men and women—and some of the best of them—are getting their call to repentance, to a new way of life, and to the conquest of self in this way, and a good many older men are superimposing a new experience on that of their youth.

Other things being equal, a solidaristic religious experience is more distinctively Christian than an individualistic religious experience. To be afraid of hell or purgatory and desirous of a life without pain or trouble in heaven was not in itself Christian. It was self-interest on a higher level. It is not strange that men were wholly intent on saving themselves as long as such dangers as Dante describes were real to their minds. A man might be pardoned for forgetting his entire social consciousness if he found himself dangling over a blazing pit. But even in more spiritual forms of conversion, as long as men are wholly intent on their own destiny, they do not necessarily emerge from selfishness. It only changes its form. A Christian regeneration must have an outlook toward humanity and result in a higher social consciousness.

The saint of the future will need not only a theocentric mysticism which enables him to realize God, but an anthropocentric mysticism which enables him to realize his fellow-men in God. The more we approach pure Christianity, the more will the Christian signify a man who loves mankind with a religious passion and excludes none. The feeling which Jesus had when he said, "I am the hungry, the naked, the lonely," will be in the emotional consciousness of all holy men in the coming days. The sense of solidarity is one of the distinctive marks of the true followers of Jesus.

Notes

1. I have set this forth fully in my little book, *Dare We Be Christians?* (Boston: Pilgrim Press, 1914). In my *Prayers of the Social Awakening* (Boston: Pilgrim Press, 1910), I have tried to connect the social consciousness with the devotional life by prayers envisioning social groups and movements. Professor Herrmann's *The Communion of the Christian with God* (London: Williams & Norgate, 1906) deals with the difference of the mystic way and the way of service.

2. Josiah Royce, *Problem of Christianity* (New York: Macmillan, 1913), I:400.

From Chapter XI

The Salvation of the Super-Personal Forces

In discussing the doctrine of sin, we faced the fact that redemption will have to deal not only with the weakness of flesh and blood, but with the strength of principalities and powers.[1] Beyond the feeble and short-lived individual towers the social group as a super-personal entity, dominating the individual, assimilating him to its moral standards, and enforcing [those standards] by the social sanctions of approval or disapproval.

When these super-personal forces are based on an evil principle, or directed toward an evil purpose, or corrupted by some controlling group interest which is hostile to the common good, they are sinners of a sublimer mould, and they block the way of redemption. They are to us what demonic personalities were to earlier Christian minds. Men of religious vision have always seen social communities in that way. The prophets dealt with Israel and Judah, with Moab and Assyria, as with personalities having a continuous life and spirit and destiny. Jesus saw Jerusalem as a man might see a beloved woman who is driven by haughtiness and self-will into tragic ruin.

In our age these super-personal social forces present more difficult problems than ever before. The scope and diversity of combination are becoming constantly greater. The strategy of the Kingdom of God is shortsighted indeed if it does not devote thought to their salvation and conversion.

*   *   *   *

The salvation of the composite personalities, like that of individuals, consists in coming under the law of Christ. A few illustrations will explain how this applies.

Two principles are contending with each other for future control in the field of industrial and commercial organization, the capitalistic and the cooperative. The effectiveness of the capitalistic method in the production of wealth is not questioned; modern civilization is evidence of it. But we are also familiar with capitalistic methods in the production of human wreckage. Its one-sided control of economic power tempts to exploitation and oppression; it directs the productive process of society primarily toward the creation of private profit rather than the service of human needs; it demands autocratic management and strengthens the autocratic principle in all social affairs; it has impressed a materialistic spirit on our whole civilization.

On the other hand, organizations formed on the cooperative principle are not primarily for profit but for the satisfaction of human wants, and the aim is to distribute ownership, control, and economic benefits to a large number of cooperators.

The difference between a capitalistic organization and a cooperative comes out clearly in the distribution of voting power. Capitalistic joint stock companies work on the plan of "one share, one vote." Therewith power is located in money. One crafty person who has a hundred shares can outvote ninety-nine righteous men who have a share apiece, and a small minority can outvote all the rest if it holds a majority of stock. Money is stronger than life, character, and personality.

Co-operatives work on the plan of "one man, one vote." A man who holds one share has as much voting power as a man with ten shares; his personality counts. If a man wants to lead and direct, he cannot do it by money power; he must do it by character, sobriety, and good judgment. The small stockholders are not passive; they take part; they must be persuaded and taught. The superior ability of the capable cannot outvote the rest, but has to train them. Consequently, the co-operatives develop men and educate a community in helpful loyalty and comradeship. This is the advent of true democracy in economic life. Of course, the co-operative principle is not a sovereign specific; the practical success of a given association depends on good judgment and the loyalty of its constituents. But the co-operatives, managed by plain men, often with little experience, have not only held their own in Europe against the picked survivors of the capitalistic competitive battle, but have forged steadily ahead into enormous financial totals, have survived and increased even during the war, and by their helpful moral influence have gone a long way to restore a country like Ireland which had long been drained and ruined by capitalism.

Here, I think, we have the difference between saved and unsaved organizations. The one class is under the law of Christ, the other under the law of mammon. The one is democratic and the other autocratic. Whenever capitalism has invaded a new country or industry, there has been a speeding up in labor and in the production of wealth, but always with a trail of human misery, discontent, bitterness, and demoralization. When co-operation has invaded a country there has been increased thrift, education, and neighborly feeling, and there has been no trail of concomitant evil and no cries of protest. The men in capitalistic business may be the best of men, far superior in ability to the average committee member of a co-operative, but the latter type of organization is the higher, and when co-operation has had as long a time to try out its methods as capitalism, the latter will rank with feudalism as an evil memory of mankind.

Super-personal forces are saved when they come under the law of Christ. A State which uses its terrible power of coercion to smite and crush offenders as a protection to the rest is still under brutal law. A State which deals with those who have erred in the way of teaching, discipline, and restoration has come under the law of Christ and is to that extent a saved community. "By their fruits ye shall know them." States are known by their courts and prisons and contract labor systems, or by their juvenile courts and parole systems. A change in penology may be an evidence of salvation.

A State which uses its superior power to overrun a weaker neighbor by force, or to wrest a valuable right of way from it by instigating a *coup d'état*, or uses intimidation to secure mining or railway concessions or to force a loan at usurious rates on a half-civilized State, is in mortal sin. A State which asks only for an open door and keeps its own door open in return, and which speaks as courteously to a backward State as to one with a big fleet, is to that extent a Christian community.[2]

*   *   *   *

With composite personalities as with individuals "the love of money is the root of all evil." Communities and nations fall into wild fits of anger and cruelty; they are vain and contemptuous of others; they lie and love lies; they sin against their critical conscience; they fall in love with virile and magnetic men just as women do. These are the temptations and dangers which every democracy will meet and from which it will recover with loss and some shame. But, as has been said before, evils become bold and permanent when there is money in them. It was the need of protecting wealth against poverty which made the courts and the criminal law so cruel in the past. It was theological superstition which started the epidemic of witch trials in Europe, but it was the large fees that fell to the lawyers and informers which made that craze so enduring.

Nearly all modern wars have had their origin in the covetousness of trade and finance.[3]

If unearned gain is the chief corrupter of professions, institutions, and combinations of men, these super-personal beings will be put on the road to salvation when their graft is in some way cut off and they are compelled to subsist on the reward of honest service.

The history of the Church furnishes a striking example. For generations before the Reformation the condition of the Church and of the ministry was the sorest social question of the time, weighing heavily on the conscience of all good men. The ministrations of the Church, the sacrament of the altar, the merit gained by the sacrifice of the mass, the penitential system, the practice of indulgences, had been turned into means of great income to the Church and those who were in control of it. The rank and file of the priests and monks were from the common people, and their incomes were poor. But the higher positions of the Church and the wealthier monasteries were in possession of the upper classes, who filled the lucrative places with their younger sons or unmarried daughters. Where rich sinecures existed and an immense patronage was in the gift of the higher churchmen, the rake-off was naturally practised and perfected. Everyone who had paid for getting his position recouped his investment. The highest institution of service had become the most glaring example of graft. Since the Church always resisted the interference of the laity, and since the oligarchy which surrounded the papacy was itself the chief beneficiary of the ecclesiastical graft, reform was successfully blocked out, or quickly lapsed when it was attempted.

It was this profit system in the Church which produced the religious unrest and finally the revolutionary upheaval of the Reformation in some nations. Men were not dissatisfied with the doctrines of the Church. There were surprisingly few theological heretics. Wycliffe and his followers are the only ones that gained popular influence, and his chief interest, too, was in the social utilization of the wealth of the Church. Men like Savonarola were not doctrinal reformers, but were trying to cleanse the Church of its graft and the resulting idleness and vice. The ideal of "the poverty of the Church," which was common to men so unlike as Saint Bernard, Arnold of Brescia, Saint Francis, and all the democratic sects, must be understood over against the vested wealth, the graft, and the semigovernmental power of the Church. They wanted the Church voluntarily to give up its wealth, and to put its ministers on the basis of service and the daily bread.

The Church refused to take this heroic path of repentance of its own free will. So it was compelled to take it. In all the countries which officially adopted the Reformation, the possessions and vested incomes of the Church were secularized. The sinecures mostly disappeared. The bishops lost their governmental functions. Everywhere the reform movements converged on this impoverishment of the Church with a kind of collective instinct. Luther's theses on indulgences got their popularity not by their new and daring theology, for they were a hesitating and wavering statement of a groping mind,— but by the fact that they touched one of the chief sources of papal income. Several of the great doctrines of the Reformation got their vitality by their internal connection with the question of church property.

The process of reformation which stripped the Church of its landed wealth and privileges was nothing beautiful. It was high-class looting. Only a small portion of the wealth was used to endow education and charity. Most of it was seized by kings, princes, and nobles. This gave a new lease of life to autocracy, and in England set up some of the splendid aristocratic families, who still consume what was once given to God. But this unholy procedure did cleanse the Church and its ministry of graft. When there were few large incomes, the rake-off perforce ceased. A body of ministers developed who were on the whole educated, clean, and willing to serve to the best of their understanding on a meagre salary. A great profession had been saved. Its salvation did not come from theology, as theology would have us believe. Where the Roman Catholic clergy is on the basis of hard work and plain income, it has shown similar improvement. The remedy which purified the ministry and the Church "so as by fire" was that "poverty of the Church" which the medieval reformers had demanded. The average minister will not be in doubt that he has married the Lady Poverty, and that this keeps him from wantonness.

The salvation of the super-personal beings is by coming under the law of Christ. The fundamental step of repentance and conversion for professions and organizations is to give up monopoly power and the incomes derived from legalized extortion, and to come under the law of service, content with a fair income for honest work. The corresponding step in the case of governments and political oligarchies, both in monarchies and in capitalistic semi-democracies, is to submit to real democracy. Therewith they step out of the Kingdom of Evil into the Kingdom of God.

Notes

1. Chapter VIII.

2. This matter of saving the community life has been discussed more fully in my book *Christianizing the Social Order* (New York: Macmillan, 1912).

3. See historical instances in F. C. Howe, *Why War?* (New York: Charles Scribner's Sons, 1916).

From Chapter XII

The Church as the Social Factor of Salvation

What is the function of the Church in the process of salvation? What is it worth to a man to have the support and guidance of the Church in saving his soul?

If we listen to the Church's own estimate of itself, it is worth as much as oxygen is to animal life. It is indispensable. "Outside of the Church there is no salvation." Very early in its history the Church began to take a deep interest in itself and to assert high things about itself. Every community is inclined to develop an expanded self-consciousness if the opportunity is at all favorable, and the Christian Church has certainly not let its opportunity go begging. Some historian has said, it is a wonder that the Church has not been made a person in the Godhead.

It is important to remember that when its high claims were first developed, they were really largely true. Christianity was in sharp opposition not only to the State but to the whole social life surrounding it. It created a Christian duplicate of the social order for its members, as far as it could. Christian influences were not yet diffused in society and literature. The Christian spirit and tradition could really be found nowhere except in the organized Christian groups. If the individual was to be impregnated with the saving power of Christianity, the Church had to do it. There was actually no salvation outside of the Church. But the statements in which men of the first generations expressed their genuine experience of what the Church meant to them were turned into a theological formula and repeated in later times when the situation had changed, and when, for a time, the Church was not the supreme help but a great hindrance. The claims for the indispensability of the Church and its sacraments and officers became more specific as the hierarchic Church developed. First, no man could be saved outside of the Church; next, he could not be saved unless he was in right relation to his bishop; and finally, he could not be saved unless he submitted to the Roman pontiff.

*   *   *   *

What are the functions of the Church in salvation, and how indispensable is it? And what has the social gospel to say to the theological valuation of the Church?

The Church is the social factor in salvation. It brings social forces to bear on evil. It offers Christ not only many human bodies and minds to serve as ministers of his salvation, but its own composite personality, with a collective memory stored with great hymns and Bible stories and deeds of heroism, with trained aesthetic and moral feelings, and with a collective will set on righteousness. A super-personal being organized around an evil principle and set on predatory aims is the most potent breeder of sin in individuals and in other communities. What, then, might a super-personal being do which would be organized around Jesus Christ as its impelling power, and would have for its sole or chief object to embody his spirit in its life and to carry him into human thought and the conduct of affairs?

If there had never been such an organization as the Christian Church, every great religious mind would dream of the possibility of creating something like it. He would imagine the happy life within it where men shared the impulses of love and the convictions about life which Jesus imparted to humanity. If he understood psychology and social science, he would see the possibilities of such a social group in arousing and guiding the unformed spiritual aspirations of the young and reinforcing wayward consciences by the approval or disapproval of the best persons, and its power of reaching by free loyalty springs of action and character lying too deep for civil law and even for education to stir. He might well imagine too how the presence of such a social group would quicken and balance the civil and political community.

How far the actualities of church life fall short of such an ideal forecast, most of us know but too well. But even so, the importance of the social factor in salvation is clear from whatever angle we look at it. What chance would a disembodied spirit of Christianity have, whispering occasionally at the keyhole of the human heart? Nothing lasts unless it is organized, and if it is organized of human life, we must put up with the qualities of human life in it.

Within the field it has chosen to cultivate, the local church under good leadership is really a power of salvation. During the formative years of our national growth the churches gathered up the available resources of education, history, philosophy, eloquence, art, and music, and established social centres controlled by the highest possessions known to people whose other resources were the family, money, gossip, the daily paper, and the inevitable vices. The great ideas of the spiritual life—God, the soul, duty, sin, holiness, eternity— would today be wholly absent in many minds, and in most others would be but flickering lights, if the local churches did not cherish and affirm them and make them glorious and persuasive by the most effective combination of social influences ever accumulated by any organization during a history lasting for centuries and spread through many nations.

We are so accustomed to the churches that we hardly realize what a social force they exert over the minds they do influence. If we could observe a native Christian church in a pagan people, after the Christian organization is once in operation as a social organism, and is weaning families and village communities from pagan customs and assimilating them to the new ideas, we should realize better the power of conservation exerted in our own communities.[1] The new religion of Christian Science provides another chance for such a realization. It expounds a new religious book alongside of the Bible, and a new prophet alongside of Christ, and thus creates a novel religious consciousness among its own people. It has taken many nervous, unhappy, and burdened persons, and has given health to their bodies and calmness and self-control to their minds by attacking and subduing their souls with a dogmatic faith, till they learn to contradict the rheumatic facts of life and to ignore even the presence of death by looking the other way. If we could see the old churches as clearly as we see this new church, we should realize their power.

The men who stand for the social gospel have been among the most active critics of the churches because they have realized most clearly both the great needs of our social life and the potential capacities of the Church to meet them. Their criticism has been a form of compliment to the Church. I think they may yet turn out to be the apologists whom the Church most needs at present. They are best fitted to see that while the Church influences society, society has always influenced the Church, and that the Church, when it has dropped to the level of its environment, has simply yielded to the law of social gravitation. This is true of the delinquencies of the Church in past ages, which lie heavily on our minds when we want to describe the Church as the great organism of salvation. Those whose expectations are created by the claims of the Church about itself may well be profoundly disappointed when they go through some of the bad chapters of Church

History. If they have to judge it by its own absolute religious criteria as the body of Christ and the exponent of his spirit, the gap between the ideal and the reality is painful. The fact is that the Church has watered its own stock and cannot pay dividends on all the paper it has issued. It has made claims for itself to which no organization composed of humans can live up. If we see it simply as an attempt to give social expression to the life derived from Christ, we shall not feel too deeply disappointed when we see it fail. True social insight knows that its sins were always the sins of the age. If the Church was autocratic and oppressive, so were all governments. There was graft in the Church, but the feudal aristocracy was founded on graft, and it never fought it as the Church fought simony.

*   *   *   *

A fresh understanding for the indispensableness of the Church is gaining ground today in Protestant theology in spite of the increased knowledge of the past and present failures of the Church. This is an attempt to overcome the exaggerated individualism into which Protestantism was thrust by the violent reactions of the Reformation. When men were in the throes of a revolution against a Church which claimed everything, they naturally denied every claim by which the enemy could brace its authority. They denied the authority of the tradition and decrees of the Church and made the Bible the sole source of truth. They denied the doctrine of the Eucharist because the mass was the chief monopoly right from which the Church drew material income and spiritual reverence. They emphasized and elaborated the doctrine of election because it effectively eliminated the middleman in salvation; for it put man into direct contact with the source of salvation and made the decree of salvation wholly independent of any human act or church mediation. But the result of this great polemical reaction against the Church was a system of religious individualism in which the social forces of salvation were slighted, and God and the individual were almost the only realities in sight.

Of course, in actual practice the Protestant churches exercised very stout control over their members. Calvin, in a celebrated passage of the Institutes, comes close to a social appreciation of the functions of the Church:

"But, as it is now our purpose to discourse of the visible Church, let us learn, from her single title of Mother, how useful, nay, how necessary the knowledge of her is, since there is no other means of entering into life unless she conceive us in the womb and give us birth, unless she nourish us at her breasts, and, in short, keep us under her charge and government, until, divested of mortal flesh, we become like the angels.—Moreover, beyond the pale of the Church no forgiveness of sins, no salvation, can be hoped for, as Isaiah and Joel testify.—The paternal favour of God and the special evidence of spiritual life are confined to his peculiar people, and hence the abandonment of the Church is always fatal."[2]

But all of us who have had to acquire our social and historical comprehension laboriously will appreciate how little the old Protestant system stimulated and developed the understanding of the social factor in redemption.

The individualism of Reformation theology is being overcome by a new insistence on the importance of the Church. This trend of thought is not due, as in Anglican theology, to a renascence of Catholicism, but to a combination of purified Protestantism and modern social insight. I have been struck by the eminence of some of the prophets of this new solidaristic strain in theology.

Schleiermacher, in his earlier "Reden über die Religion," still interpreted the religious sense of dependence as an individual experience. Maturer reflection showed him that all personal life is determined by the spirit of the community with which it is organically connected. This is true of the religious life, too. Our sin is due to the feebleness with which we realize God. Jesus lived in complete and unbroken consciousness of

God. Contact with him can so strengthen the God-consciousness in us that we are able to overcome the power of sin and rise to newness of life. But the memory of his life and the consciousness of salvation in him are transmitted to us only by the Church. We share his consciousness by sharing the common faith and experience of the Church. The new life of the individual is mediated by the social organism which is already in possession of that life.

"The Protestant theology of our age rests on the foundation laid by Schleiermacher; all theologians—some directly, some more indirectly—are seeking to establish the connections between the religious personality of the individual and the common consciousness of the Church."[3]

Ritschl, the most vigorous and influential theological intellect in Germany since Schleiermacher, is evidence of this. He abandoned the doctrine of original sin but substituted the solidaristic conception of the Kingdom of Evil. He held that salvation is embodied in a community which has experienced salvation; the faith of the individual is part of the faith of the Church. The Church and not the individual is the object of justification; the assurance of forgiveness for the individual is based on his union with the Church.

*   *   *   *

In American thought the most striking utterance on the indispensable importance of the Church in salvation has come from an eminent outsider, a philosopher and not a theologian, Professor Royce. He had worked out "the philosophy of loyalty" in other fields, and then applied it to religion in *The Problem of Christianity* (1913). This book is the mature product of his life, and its argument is evidently uplifted by the conviction that he had discovered some highly important facts.

Professor Royce, as has been said before, held that there are in the human world two profoundly different grades or levels of mental beings, namely individuals and communities, and he calls it the most significant of all moral and religious truths "that a community, when unified by an active, indwelling purpose, is an entity more concrete and less mysterious than any individual man, and can love and be loved as a husband and wife love." What is love between man and man, becomes loyalty when it goes out from a man to his community.

Professor Royce felt profoundly on the sin of the individual. "The individual human being is by nature subject to some overwhelming moral burden, from which, if unaided, he cannot escape. Both because of what has been technically called original sin, and because of the sins that he himself has committed, the individual is doomed to a spiritual ruin from which only a divine intervention can save him" (Lecture III). He "cannot unaided win the true goal of life. Help must come to him from some source above his own level."

The individual is saved, if at all, by membership in a community which has salvation. When a man becomes loyal to a community, he identifies himself with its life; he appropriates its past history and memories, its experiences and hopes, and absorbs its spirit and faith. This is the power which can lift him above his own level.

The Christian religion possesses such a community. It first comes into full view in the Pauline epistles. How it originated is a mystery like the origin of life, for loyalty is always evoked by the loyalty of those who already have it. Paul did not create it; he only formulated its ideas.

Professor Royce thinks the creation of the Church was the most important event in the history of Christianity. Not Christ but the Church is the central idea of Christianity. He rates Jesus largely as an indispensable basis on which the Church could form and stand. He thinks we know little about him, and that Jesus defined the Christian ideas inadequately. But his name was the great symbol of loyalty for the Church. The doctrines about him were developed because they were necessary for the consolidation of the Church.

This slighting of Jesus is one of the most unsatisfactory elements in Royce's thought. If the awakening of loyalty is "a spiritual triumph beyond the wit of man"; if "you are first made loyal through the power of someone else who is loyal"; if "no social will can make the community lovable unless loyalty is previously effective"; then the origin of "the beloved community" is the great problem in the history of Christianity, and everything points to Jesus as the only solution. He performed the miracle of the origin of life. A proper evaluation of Jesus as the initiator would have been the natural and necessary consummation of this entire doctrine of salvation by loyalty.

A tacit condition is attached to all the high claims made by Professor Royce and others on behalf of the Church: If the Church is to have saving power, it must embody Christ. He is the revolutionary force within it. The saving qualities of the Church depend on the question whether it has translated the personal life of Jesus Christ into the social life of its group and thus brings it to bear on the individual. If Christ is not in the Church, how does it differ from "the world"? It will still assimilate its members, but it will not make them persons bearing the family likeness of the first-born son of God.

Wherever the Church has lost the saving influence of Christ, it has lost its saltness and is a tasteless historical survival. Therewith all theological doctrines about it become untrue. Antiquity and continuity are no substitute for the vitality of the Christ-spirit. Age, instead of being a presumption in favor of a religious body, is a question-mark set over against its name. The world is full of stale religion. It is historically self-evident that church bodies do lose the saving power. In fact, they may become social agencies to keep their people stupid, stationary, superstitious, bigoted, and ready to choke their first-born ideals and instincts as a sacrifice to the God of stationariness whom their religious guides have imposed on them. Wherever an aged and proud Church sets up high claims

as an indispensable institution of salvation, let it be tested by
the cleanliness, education, and moral elasticity of the agricultural labourers whom it has long controlled, or of the slum
dwellers who have long ago slipped out of its control.

This conditional form of predicating the saving power and
spiritual authority of the Church is only one more way of
asserting that in anything which claims to be Christian, religion
must have an immediate ethical nexus and effect. This marks
an essential difference between the claims made for the Church
in Catholic theology and the emphasis on the functions of the
Church made in the social gospel. The Catholic doctrine of
the Church made its holiness, its power to forgive sin, and the
efficacy of its sacraments independent of the moral character
of its priests and people; the social conception makes everything conditional on the spiritual virtues of the church group.
The Catholic conception stakes the claims of the Church and
its clergy on the due legal succession and canonical ordination
of its chief officers. This imports legal conceptions derived
from the imperial Roman bureaucracy into the organism of
the Christian Church, which has nothing to do with any bureaucracy. It gives an unquestioned status to some corrupt,
venal, or ignorant bishop in Southern Italy; makes the ecclesiastical validity of the entire Anglican clergy dubious; and
denies all standing to Chalmers, Spurgeon, or Asbury. The
social gospel, on the other hand, tests the claims and powers
of any Church by the continuity of the apostolic faith within
it and by its possession of the law and spirit of Jesus.

The saving power of the Church does not rest on its institutional character, on its continuity, its ordination, its ministry,
or its doctrine. It rests on the presence of the Kingdom of God
within her. The Church grows old; the Kingdom is ever young.
The Church is a perpetuation of the past; the Kingdom is the
power of the coming age. Unless the Church is vitalized by
the ever-nascent forces of the Kingdom within her, she deadens
instead of begetting.

Notes

1. *Social Christianity in the Orient*, by Emma Rauschenbusch Clough, Ph.D. (New York: Macmillan, 1914) is a striking narrative of the revolutionary effect of the introduction of Christianity in an Indian pariah tribe.

2. John Calvin, *Institutes of the Christian Religion*, Book IV, i, 4.

3. Otto Pfleiderer, *Grundriss der* Christlichen *Glaubens- und Sittenlehre* (Berlin: G. Reimer, 1880), § 55.

Walter Rauschenbusch, On Prayer

Selections from *Prayers of the Social Awakening*

Against War

Lord, since first the blood of Abel cried to thee from the ground that drank it, this earth of thine has been defiled with the blood of man shed by his brother's hand, and the centuries sob with the ceaseless horror of war. Ever the pride of kings and the covetousness of kings have driven peaceful nations to slaughter. Ever the songs of the past and pomp of armies have been used to inflame the passions of the people. Our spirit cries out to thee in revolt against it, and we know that our righteous anger is answered by thy holy wrath.

Break thou the spell of the enchantments that make the nations drunk with the lust of battle and draw them on as willing tools of death. Grant us a quiet and steadfast mind when our own nation clamors for vengeance or aggression. Strengthen our sense of justice and our regard for the equal worth of other peoples and races. Grant to the rulers of nations faith in the possibility of peace through justice, and grant to the common people a new and stern enthusiasm for the cause of peace. Bless our soldier and sailors for their swift obedience and their willingness to answer to the call of duty, but inspire them nonetheless with a hatred of war, and may

they never for the love of private glory or advancement pro-
mote its coming. May our young men rejoice to die for their
country with the valor of their fathers, but teach our age nobler
methods of matching our strength and more effective ways of
giving our life for the flag.

O thou strong Father of all nations, draw all thy family
together with an increasing sense of our common blood and
destiny, that peace may come on earth at last, and thy sun may
shed its light rejoicing on a holy brotherhood of peoples.

Against Alcoholism

Lord, we praise thy holy name, for thou hast made bare thine arm in the sight of all nations and done wonders. But still we cry to thee in the weary struggle of our people against the power of drink. Remember, Lord, the strong men who were led astray and blighted in the flower of their youth. Remember the aged who have brought their gray hairs to a dishonored grave. Remember the homes that have been made desolate of joy, the wifely love that has been outraged in its sanctuary, the little children who have learned to despise when once they loved. Remember, O thou great avenger of sin, and make this nation to remember.

May those who now entrap the feet of the weak and make their living by the degradation of men, thrust away their shameful gains and stand clear. But if their conscience is silenced by profit, do thou grant thy people the indomitable strength of faith to make an end of it. May all the great churches of our land shake off those who seek the shelter of religion for that which damns, and stand level front against their common foe. May all those who still soothe their souls with half-truths, saying "Peace, peace," where there can be no peace, learn to see through thy stern eyes and come to the help of Jehovah against the mighty. Help us to cast down the men in high places who use the people's powers to beat back the people's hands from the wrong they fain to crush.

O God, bring nigh the day when all our men shall face their daily task with minds undrugged and with tempered passions; when the unseemly mirth of drink shall seem a shame to all who hear and see; when the trade that debauches men shall be loathed like the trade that debauches women; and when all this black remnant of savagery shall haunt the memory of a new generation but as an evil dream of the night. For this accept our vows, O Lord, and grant thine aid.

Against the Servants of Mammon

We cry to thee for justice, O Lord, for our soul is weary with the inequity of greed. Behold the servants of Mammon, who defy thee and drain their fellow-men for gain; who grind down the strength of workers by merciless toil and fling them aside when they are mangled and worn; who rack-rent the poor and make dear the space and air which thou hast made free; who paralyze the hand of justice by corruption and blind the eyes of the people by lies; who nullify by their craft the merciful laws which nobler men have devised for the protection of the weak; who have made us ashamed of our dear country by their defilements and have turned our holy freedom into a hollow name; who have brought upon thy Church the contempt of men and have cloaked their extortion with the Gospel of thy Christ.

For the oppression of the poor and the sighing of the needy now do thou arise, O Lord; for because thou art love, and tender as a mother to the weak, therefore thou art the great hater of iniquity and thy doom is upon those who grow rich on the poverty of the people.

O God, we are afraid, for the thundercloud of thy wrath is even now black above us. In the ruins of dead empires we have read how thou hast trodden the wine-press of thine anger when the measure of their sin was full. We are sick at heart when we remember that by the greed of those who enslaved a weaker race that curse was fastened upon us all which still lies black and hopeless across our land, though the blood of a nation was spilled to stone. Save our people from being dragged down into vaster guilt and woe by men who have no vision and know no law except their lust. Shake their souls with awe of thee that they may cease. Help us with clean hands to tear the web which they have woven about us and to turn thy people back to thy law, lest the mark of the beast stand out on the right hand and forehead of our nation and our feet be set on the downward path of darkness from which there is no return forever.

Against Impurity

Thou whose light is about me and within me and to whom all things are present, help me this day to keep my life pure in thy sight. Suffer me not by any lawless act of mine to befoul any innocent life or add to the shame and hopelessness of any erring one that struggles faintly against sin. Grant me a steadfast scorn for pleasure brought by human degradation. May no reckless word on wanton look from me kindle the slow fires of wayward passion that will char and consume the divine beauties of any soul. Give me grace to watch over the imaginations of my heart, lest in the unknown hour of my weakness my secret thoughts leap into shame. If my friends trust me with their loved ones, save me from betraying their trust and from slaying the peace of a home. If any dear heart has staked its life and hopes on my love and loyalty, I beseech thee that its joy and strength may never wither through my forgetfulness or guilt. O God, make me pure and a helper to the weak. Grant that even the sins of my past may yield me added wisdom and tenderness to help those who are tempted.

Save our nation from the corruption that breeds corruption. Save our innocent sons and daughters from the secret curse that requites the touch of love with lingering death. O Jesus, thou master of all who are both strong and pure, take our weak and passionate hearts under thy control, that when the dusk settles on our life, we may go to our long rest with no pang of shame, and may enter into the blessedness of seeing God, which thou hast promised only to the pure in heart.

For the Kingdom of God

Christ, thou hast bidden us pray for the coming of thy Father's kingdom, in which his righteous will shall be done on earth. We have treasured thy words, but we have forgotten their meaning, and thy great hope has grown dim in thy Church. We bless thee for the inspired souls of all ages who saw afar the shining city of God, and by faith left the profit of the present to follow their vision. We rejoice that today the hope of these lonely hearts is becoming the clear faith of millions. Help us, O Lord, in the courage of faith to seize what has now come so near, that the glad day of God may dawn at last. As we have mastered Nature that we might gain wealth, help us now to master the social relations of mankind that we may gain justice and a world of brothers. For what shall it profit our nation if it gain numbers and riches, and lose the sense of the living God and the joy of human brotherhood?

Make us determined to live by truth and not by lies, to found our common life on the eternal foundations of righteousness and love, and no longer to prop the tottering house of wrong by legalized cruelty and force. Help us to make the welfare of all the supreme law of our land, that so our commonwealth may be build strong and secure on the love of all its citizens. Cast down the throne of Mammon who ever grinds the life of men, and set up thy throne, O Christ, for thou didst die that men might live. Show thy erring children at last the way from the City of Destruction to the City of Love, and fulfill the longings of the prophets of humanity. Our Master, once more we make thy faith or prayer: "Thy kingdom come! Thy will be done on earth!"

For Those Who Come After Us

O God, we pray thee for those who come after us, for our children of our friends, and for all the young lives that are marching up from the gates of birth, pure and eager, with the morning sunshine on their faces. We remember with a pang that these will live in the world we are making for them. We are wasting the resources of the earth in our headlong greed, and they will suffer want. We are building sunless houses and joyless cities for our profit, and they must dwell therein. We are making the burden heavy and the pace of work pitiless, and they will fall wan and sobbing by the wayside. We are poisoning the air of our land by our lies and our uncleanness, and they will breathe it.

O God, thou knowest how we have cried out in agony when the sins of our fathers have been visited upon us, and how we have struggled vainly against the inexorable fate that coursed in our blood or bound us in a prison-house of life. Save us from maiming the innocent ones who come after us by the added cruelty of our sins. Help us to break the ancient force of evil by a holy and steadfast will and to endow our children with purer blood and nobler thoughts. Grant us grace to leave the earth fairer than we found it; to build upon it cities of God in which the cry of needless pain shall cease; and to put the yoke of Christ upon our business life that it may serve and not destroy. Lift the veil of the future and show us the generation to come as it will be if blighted by our guilt, that our lust may be cooled and we may walk in the fear of the Eternal. Grant us a vision of the far-off years as they may be if redeemed by the sons of God, that we may take heart and do battle for thy children and ours.

On the Harm We Have Done

Our Father, we look back on the years that are gone and shame and sorrow come upon us, for the harm we have done to others, for the harm we have done to others rises up in our memory to accuse us. Some we have seared with the fire of our lust, and some we have scorched by the heat of our anger. In some we helped to squelch the glow of young ideals by our selfish pride and craft, and in some we have nipped the opening bloom of our faith by the frost of our unbelief.

We might have followed our blessed footsteps, O Christ, binding up the bruised hearts of our brothers and guiding the wayward passions of the young to firmer manhood. Instead, there are poor hearts now broken and darkened because they encountered us on the way, and some perhaps remember us only as the beginning of their misery or sin.

O God, we know that all our prayers can never bring back the past, and no tears can wash out the red marks with which we have scarred some life that stands before our memory with accusing eyes. Grant that at least a humble and pure life may grow out of our late contrition, that in the brief days still left to us we may comfort and heal where we have scorned and crushed. Change us by the power of our saving grace from sources of evil into forces for good, that with all our strength we may fight the wrongs we have aided, and aid the right we have clogged. Grant us this boon, that for every harm we have done, we may do some brave act of salvation, and that for every soul that has stumbled or fallen through us, we may bring to thee some other weak or despairing one, whose strength has been renewed by our love, that so the face of the Christ may smile upon us and the light within us may shine undimmed.

For the Prophets and Pioneers

We praise thee, Almighty God, for thine elect, the prophets and martyrs of humanity, who gave their thoughts and prayers and agonies for the truth of God and the freedom of the people. We praise thee that amid loneliness and the contempt of men, in poverty and imprisonment, when they were condemned by the laws of the mighty and buffeted on the scaffold, thou didst uphold them by thy spirit in loyalty to thy holy cause.

Our hearts burn within us as we follow the bleeding feet of thy Christ down the centuries, and count the mounts of anguish on which he was crucified anew in his prophets and the true apostles of his spirit. Help us to forgive those who did it, for some truly thought they were serving thee when they suppressed thy light, but oh, save us from the same mistake! Grant us an unerring instinct for what is right and true, and a swift sympathy to divine those who truly love and serve the people. Suffer us not by thoughtless condemnation or selfish opposition to weaken the arm and chill the spirit of those who strive for the redemption of mankind. May we never bring upon us the blood of all the righteous by renewing the spirit of those who persecuted them in the past. Grant us rather that we, too, may be counted in the chosen band of those who have given their life as a ransom for the many. Send us forth with the pathfinders of humanity to lead thy people another day's march toward the land of promise.

And if we, too, must suffer loss, and drink of the bitter pool of misunderstanding and scorn, uphold us by thy spirit in steadfastness and joy because we are found worthy to share in the work and the reward of Jesus and all the saints.

Dorothy Day, On the Founding of the Catholic Worker

Selections from *The Long Loneliness: The Autobiography of the Legendary Catholic Social Activist*

Paper, People, and Work

We started publishing *The Catholic Worker* at 436 East Fifteenth Street (now at 39 Spring Street) in May, 1933, with a first issue of 2,500 copies. Within three or four months the circulation bounded to 25,000, and it was cheaper to bring it out as an eight-page tabloid on newsprint rather than the smaller-sized edition on better paper we had started with. By the end of the year we had a circulation of 100,000, and by 1936 it was 150,000. It was certainly a mushroom growth. It was not only that some parishes subscribed for the paper all over the country in bundles of 500 or more. Zealous young people took the paper out in the streets and sold it, and when they could not sell it even at one cent a copy, they gave free copies and left them in streetcar, bus, barber shop, and dentist's and doctor's office. We got letters from all parts of the country from people who said they had picked up the paper on trains, in rooming houses. One letter came from the state of Sonora in Mexico, and we read with amazement that the reader had tossed in an uncomfortable bed on a hot night until he got up to turn over the mattress and under it found a copy of *The Catholic Worker*. A miner found a copy five miles underground in an old mine that stretched out under the Atlantic Ocean off Nova Scotia. A seminarian said that he had sent out his shoes to be half-soled in Rome, and they came back to him wrapped in a copy of *The Catholic Worker*. These letters thrilled and inspired the young people who came to help, sent by Brothers or Sisters who taught in the high schools. We were invited to speak in schools and parishes, and often as a result of our speaking others came in to help us. On May Day, those first few years, the streets were literally lined with papers. Looking back on it, it seemed like a gigantic advertising campaign, entirely unpremeditated. It grew organically, Peter used to say happily, and not through organization. "We are not an organization, we are an organism," he said.

First there was Peter, my brother, and I. When John took a job at Dobb's Ferry, a young girl, Dorothy Weston, who had been studying journalism and was a graduate of a Catholic college, came to help. She lived at home and spent her days with us, eating with us and taking only her carfare from the common fund. Peter brought in three young men from Columbus Circle, whom he had met when discussing the affairs of the world there, and of these one became bookkeeper (that was his occupation when he was employed), another circulation manager, and the third married Dorothy Weston. Another girl came to take dictation and help with mailing the paper, and she married the circulation manager. There were quite a number of romances that first year—the paper appealed to youth. Then there were the young intellectuals who formed what they called Campion Committees in other cities as well as New York, who helped to picket the Mexican and German consulates and who distributed literature all over the city. Workers came in to get help on picket lines, to help move dispossessed families and make demonstrations in front of relief offices. Three men came to sell the paper on the street, and to eat their meals with us. Big Dan had been a truck driver and a policeman. The day he came in to see us he wanted nothing more than to bathe his tired feet. That night at supper

Peter indoctrinated him on the dignity of poverty and read some of Father Vincent McNabb's *Nazareth or Social Chaos*. This did not go over so well, all of us being city people, and Father McNabb advocating a return to the fields, but he made Dan Orr go out with a sense of a mission, not worrying about shabby clothes or the lack of a job. Dan began to sell the paper on the streets and earned enough money to live on. He met others who had found subsistence jobs, carrying sandwich signs or advertising children's furniture by pushing a baby carriage, a woman who told fortunes in a tea shop, a man who sold pretzels, which were threaded on four poles one on each corner of an old baby carriage. He found out their needs, and those of their families, and never left the house in the morning without bundles of clothes as well as his papers.

Dan rented a horse and wagon in which to deliver bundles of the paper each month. (We had tried this before he came, but someone had to push the horse while the other led it. We knew nothing about driving a wagon.) Dan loved his horse. He called it Catholic Action, and used to take the blanket off my bed to cover the horse in winter. We rented it from a German Nazi on East Sixteenth Street, and sometimes when we had no money he let us have the use of it free for a few hours. It rejoiced our hearts to move a Jewish family into their new quarters with his equipment.

Dan said it was a pious horse and that when he passed St. Patrick's Cathedral, the horse genuflected. He liked to drive up Fifth Avenue, preferably with students who had volunteered their help, and shout, "Read *The Catholic Worker*" at the top of his lungs. He was anything but dignified and loved to affront the dignity of others.

One time he saw me coming down the street when he was selling the paper in front of Gimbel's and began to yell, "Read *The Catholic Worker!* Romance on every page." A seminarian from St. Louis, now Father Dreisoner, took a leaf from Dan's book and began selling the paper on the corner of Times Square and at union meetings. He liked to stand next to a comrade selling *The Daily Worker,* and as the one shouted, "Read *The Daily Worker,*" he in turn shouted, "Read *The Catholic Worker* daily." Between sales they conversed.

Another of Peter's friends was an old Armenian who wrote poetry in a beautiful mysterious script which delighted my eyes. He carried his epic around with him always. He was very little and wore a long black overcoat which reached to his heels and a black revolutionary hat over his long white hair. He had a black cat whom he called Social Justice, mimicking Big Dan. She was his constant companion. He used my washrag to wipe her face with after eating. He prepared dishes for us with rice and meat wrapped in grape leaves, held together with toothpicks. He slept on a couch in the kitchen for a time. Once when Tamar was tearing around the house playing with Freddy Rubino, the little boy who lived upstairs, and I told her to be a little more quiet, that Mr. Alinas was asleep in the next room, she said mischievously, "I don't care if the Pope is asleep in the next room, we want to play and make noise." Day and night there were many meetings in the converted barber shop which was our office, and Tamar heard plenty of noise from us. When someone asked her how she liked *The Catholic Worker* she wrinkled up her nose and said she liked the farming-commune idea, but that there was too much talk about all the rest.

Peter, the "green" revolutionist, had a long-term program which called for hospices, or houses of hospitality, where the works of mercy could be practiced to combat the taking over by the state of all those services which could be built up by mutual aid; and farming communes to provide land and homes for the unemployed, whom increasing technology was piling up into the millions. In 1933, the unemployed numbered 13,000,000.

The idea of the houses of hospitality caught on quickly enough. The very people that Peter brought in, who made up our staff at first, needed a place to live. Peter was familiar with the old I.W.W. technique of a common flophouse and a pot of mulligan on the stove. To my cost, I too had become well acquainted with this idea.

Besides, we never had any money, and the cheapest, most practical way to take care of people was to rent some apartments and have someone do the cooking for the lot of us. Many a time I was cook and cleaner as well as editor and street seller. When Margaret, a Lithuanian girl from the mining regions of Pennsylvania came to us and took over the cooking, we were happy indeed. She knew how to make a big pot of mashed potatoes with mushroom sauce which filled everyone up nicely. She was a great soft creature with a little baby, Barbara, who was born a few months after she came to us. Margaret went out on May Day with the baby and sold papers on the street. She loved being propagandist as well as cook. When Big Dan teased her, she threatened to tell the "pasture" of the church around the corner.

To house the women, we had an apartment near First Avenue which could hold about ten. When there were arguments among them, Margaret would report them with gusto, giving us a blow-by-blow account. Once when she was telling how one of the women abused her so that she "felt as though the crown of thorns was pressing right down on her head" (she was full of these mystical experiences), Peter paused in his pacing of the office to tell her she needed to scrub the kitchen floor. Not that he was ever harsh, but he was making a point that manual labor was the cure of all such quarreling. Margaret once told Bishop O'Hara of Kansas City that when she kissed his ring, it was just like a blood transfusion—she got faint all over.

Jacques Maritain came to us during these early days and spoke to the group, who were reading *Freedom and the Modern World* at that time. He gave special attention to the chapter on the purification of means. Margaret was delighted with our distinguished guest, who so evidently loved us all, and made him a box of fudge to take home with him when he sailed for France a few weeks later.

Ah, those early days that everyone likes to think of now since we have grown so much bigger; that early zeal, that early romance, that early companionableness! And how delightful it is to think that the young ones who came into the work now find the same joy in community. It is a permanent revolution, this Catholic Worker Movement.

In New York we were soon forced by the increasing rent of three apartments and one store to move into a house on the West Side. We lived on West Charles Street, all together, men and women, students and workers, about twenty of us. In the summer young college girls and men came for months to help us, and, in some cases, returned to their own cities to start houses of hospitality there. In this way, houses started in Boston, Rochester, Milwaukee, and other cities. Within a few years there were thirty-three houses of hospitality and farms around the country.

One of the reasons for the rapid growth was that many young men were coming out of college to face the prospect of no job. If they had started to read *The Catholic Worker* in college, they were ready to spend time as volunteers when they came out. Others were interested in writing, and houses in Buffalo, Chicago, Baltimore, Seattle, St. Louis, and Philadelphia, to name but a few cities, published their own papers and sold them with the New York *Catholic Worker*. A *Catholic Worker* was started in Australia and one in England. Both papers are still in existence, but the New York *Catholic Worker* is the only one published in the United States. The English and Australian papers are neither pacifist nor libertarian in their viewpoint, but the Australian paper is decentralist as well as strongly pro-labor. The English paper concentrates on labor organization and legislation. "These papers have part of the program," Peter said, "but ours makes a synthesis—with vision."

The coming of war closed many of the houses of hospitality, but with new ones reopening there are still more than twenty houses and farms. When the young men in the work were released from service, most of them married and had to think in terms of salaries, jobs to support their growing families. The voluntary apostolate was for the unwilling celibate and for the unemployed as well as for the men and women, willing celibates, who felt that running hospices, performing the works of mercy, working on farms, was their vocation, just as definitely a vocation as that of the professed religious.

Voluntary poverty means a good deal of discomfort in these houses of ours. Many of the houses throughout the country are without central heating and have to be warmed by stoves in winter. There are backyard toilets for some even now. The first Philadelphia house had to use water drawn from one spigot at the end of an alley, which served half a dozen other houses. It was lit with oil lamps. It was cold and damp and so unbelievably poverty-stricken that little children coming to see who the young people meeting there were exclaimed that this could not be a *Catholic* place; it was too poor. We must be Communists. They were well acquainted with the Communist point of view, since they were Puerto Rican and Spanish and Mexican, and this was at the beginning of the Spanish Civil War.

How hard a thing it is to hear such criticisms made. Voluntary poverty was only found among the Communists; the Negro and white man on the masthead of our paper suggested communism; the very word "worker" made people distrust us at first. We were not taking the position of the great mass of Catholics, who were quite content with the present in this world. They were quite willing to give to the poor, but they did not feel called upon to work for the things of this life for others which they themselves esteemed so lightly. Our insistence on worker-ownership, on the right of private property, on the need to de-proletarize the worker, all points which had been emphasized by the popes in their social encyclicals, made many Catholics thank we were Communists in disguise, wolves in sheep's clothing.

The house on Mott Street which we occupied for many years began to loom up in our lives as early as 1934, through

Mary Lane. She was one of our readers, who lived in a small tenement apartment on the upper West Side on her telegrapher's pension. She was very holy, and when she first saw a copy of the paper with its stories of human misery, she who also saw poverty at firsthand, began collecting clothes for us. The first time she came down she stood at the door dramatically and said to me abruptly, "Do you have ecstasies and visions?" Poor dear, so hungry for mystical experience, even if secondhand, after a long life of faith.

I was taken aback. "Visions of unpaid bills," I said abruptly. Her warmth, her effusiveness, were embarrassing but I soon learned to take them for what they were, an overflowing of an ardent soul, ready to pour itself out in love.

She became our faithful friend. She was lame, half blind, old, yet she stinted herself and gave us five dollars a month of her pension. She had a well-to-do friend named Gertrude Burke, the only daughter of an invalid widowed mother. Gertrude took care of her mother until she died and then began to give her property away to the Church. She went to live at the House of Calvary, a cancer hospital for the poor, which was one of her pet charities. This had been founded by a small group of widows, a "lay institute" according to the terminology of the Church. They were not a religious order. Neither wife nor virgin could belong, though either could help. Miss Burke's uptown house was given to the order of the Good Shepherd. The house on Mott Street had been built by an old uncle back in 1860. His name was Kerrigan, and it was said he had defended old St. Patrick's Cathedral on Mott Street during the Know Nothing riots, standing on the steps with a gun in his hand.

At 115 Mott Street, there was a rear house which had been the original house, and had had a long yard in front; there also was the front house, twice as deep, four rooms on either side of a long narrow hall. The rear house had two rooms on either side with one toilet between them, open fireplaces, a sink, and a washtub in each kitchen. In these primitive, unheated, bathless flats, made up of a kitchen and bedroom, the Irish first came to live and then the Italians. Katie, the vegetable woman on the corner, told me her mother had lived on the first floor of the rear building and that St. Francis Cabrini had visited her there. That two-room flat was dark and airless, surrounded as it was by five-story buildings on every side. The sun never reached the rear room, whose long window looked out on another five-story building, one foot away. Yet when the priest came to read the prayers for the dying in that dark room, a ray of sunlight fell on his book so that the candle held by Katie herself was no longer needed!

This entire rear house was empty when I first saw it. Half of the apartments in the front building were also empty. Miss Burke offered us the use of the empty apartments provided we would collect the rents on the rest and be caretakers. It was so much worse a neighborhood than Fifteenth Street that I was appalled at the idea. I asked Rose Clafani, whom I met on the stairs, if she had lived there long, and she said stormily, "I was born in this g—d— place!" And that was all I got out of her! I found afterward that she was afraid we were going to buy the building and evict them, and her heart was there. She loved her home.

I turned down the offer then, but within a few years I regretted it. I felt it was wrong to take rent for such a place—that it had far better be tom down, or given rent free to the poor. I might easily have expressed myself along these lines, so imprudent am I, so hasty in speech.

When we had found the house on Charles Street too small for us, I telephoned Mary Lane and asked her to intercede for us with Miss Burke, to tell her that we had reconsidered and would be most grateful for the use of the rear house at 125 Mott Street. We would not, however, collect rents on the front building. There was one store empty at that time, and we asked for that too. Miss Burke reminded us of the fact that we refused the house when we could have had it—we had not understood her previous offer in this way—and that now she had given the place to the House of Calvary. However, she would ask them if we could use it. The housing crisis was not on us at that time. So, finally we obtained the use of the house and moved in. The other store in front was a speakeasy, run as a dry-goods store. When the tenants moved out we took that as an office. As the apartments became vacant, we rented them for eighteen dollars each. We ended by having twelve rooms in the front house for women, another four for men, which with those in the rear house made twenty-four rooms for men. Four were used for laundry and storerooms. We did not use the basement because of rats and defective plumbing. The neighbors used one cellar of the rear building for wine-making, and hogsheads of wine were stored there. Once, one of our workers, a former seaman, went down in the cellar and in trying to obtain wine, let much of it escape. We had to pay for it. These apartments and stores, on this narrow, pushcart-lined street, were our home for fourteen years.

The people who worked with us! For the first six months that we published *The Catholic Worker*, we longed for an artist who could illustrate Peter's ideas. An answer to our prayers came in the form of a young girl just out of high school who signed her work "A. de Bethune." Her woodcuts were of worker-saints, St. Peter the fisherman, St. Paul writing in prisons, walking the roads, and indoctrinating St. Timothy, St. Crispin the shoemaker, St. Conrad, and a host of minor saints, if any saints could be called minor who gave their lives for the faith, whose hearts burned with so single-hearted a fire.

"A picture," Ade reminded us, "was worth ten thousand words." Through a misunderstanding as to her name, we signed her pictures "Ade Bethune," and so she was called by all of us. She was Belgian, and it was only some years later that we knew her title, which her mother continued to use, Baronne de Bethune. The aristocrat and the peasant Peter got on famously. "Our word is tradition," he said happily, and wrote a little essay, "Shouting a Word."

Mrs. Bethune and her daughter illustrated for Peter many ideas besides *noblesse oblige*. He liked to illustrate his ideas by calling attention to people who exemplified them. The Bethune family performed all the works of mercy out of slender resources, earned by the labor of their hands. They had come to this country at the close of World War I. They exemplified voluntary poverty and manual labor and the love of neighbors to the highest degree.

When Ade built up her studio in Newport where the family moved soon after we met them, she took in apprentices, young girls from different parts of the country who could not have afforded to pay tuition or to support themselves. Two of her apprentices married and went to live on Catholic Worker farms, and are now mothers of large families. My own daughter went to her when she was sixteen and stayed a year, learning the household arts. For to Ade, as to Eric Gill and Peter Maurin, the holy man was the whole man, the man of integrity, who not only tried to change the world, but to live in it as it was.

Whenever I visited Ade I came away with a renewed zest for life. She has such a sense of the sacramentality of life, the goodness of things, a sense that is translated in all her works, whether it was illustrating a missal, making stained-glass windows or sewing, cooking or gardening. To do things perfectly was always her aim. Another first principle she always taught was to aim high. "If you are going to put a cross bar on an H," she said, "you have to aim *higher* than your sense of sight tells you."

Dom Vitry, a Benedictine monk from Mared-sous, said this same thing in regard to music: "Aim higher than the note you wish to reach, and you will come down on it."

Ade came to learn from us as well as give us her woodcuts, and we have learned from her. Peter taught her, and she translated his teachings into pictures which we used again and again in the paper.

Once I was attending a steelworker's open-air meeting in Pittsburgh, and when we had distributed the papers we brought, I was amused and delighted to see a huge Slovak or Hungarian worker pointing to the pictures of the working saints and laughing with the joy of discovery.

Ade not only drew for our paper—she allowed her work to be copied by papers all over the world, Catholic and non-Catholic. We saw reproductions of her woodcuts in Japanese papers, Portuguese papers, Indian papers, to mention but a few.

Before she was mid-twenty she had designed and with unemployed steelworkers helped build a church in the outskirts of Pittsburgh. She made the stained-glass windows in the Church of the Precious Blood in Brooklyn and recently finished mosaics in a church in the Philippines. In addition to her work of painting, carving, et cetera, she edits a Catholic art quarterly and is a trustee of St. Benedict's farm in Massachusetts, one of the Catholic Worker centers.

On that farm where four families live, one family is made up of seven boys, a father who must go out to work, and a mother who has been hospitalized for some years. Ade and her mother have helped this family, as they have helped a number of others in many ways. Not only money and clothes but hard manual labor made up their contributions. Every week a bundle of clothes was sent—and this went on for years—to the Baronne de Bethune in Newport, and she washed, ironed, and mended these clothes and sent them back.

It is wonderful to think of and to write of such good works. Hundreds of pairs of socks for men on our breadlines, funds collected—she was always the great lady with special projects into which she drew many others.

I like to speak of her nobility because in her case that is actually what the word connotes. We emphasize the "Prince" when referring to Kropotkin precisely because he gave up titles and estates to be with the poor. We can recognize too our own country's claim to greatness in that here titles are naturally discarded in an attempt to reach the highest principle of human brotherhood.

The de Bethune family lost much in World War I, but when they came here their philosophy of work was so vital that they made what Eric Gill called a cell of good living.

It is amazing how quickly one can gather together a family. Steve Hergenhan came to us from Union Square. He was a German carpenter, a skilled workman who after forty years of frugal living had bought himself a plot of ground near Suffern, New York, and had proceeded to build on it, using much of the natural rock in the neighborhood. He built his house on a hillside and used to ski down to the village to get groceries. He did not like cars and would not have one. He thought that cars were driving people to their ruin. Workers bought cars who should buy homes, he said, and they willingly sold themselves into slavery and indebtedness for the sake of the bright new shining cars that speeded along the superhighways. Maybe he refused to pay taxes for the roads that accommodated the cars. Maybe he was unable to. At any rate, he lost his little house on the side of the hill and ended up in New York, on a park bench during the day, telling his grievances to all who would listen, and eating and sleeping in the Municipal Lodging House, which then maintained the largest dormitory in the world, seven hundred double-decker beds.

Peter loved the articulate, and after having one of his "round-table discussions" with Steve in Union Square, he invited him to come and stay with us. The technique of the Square then was for two people to have a discussion together with no one interrupting until he was given permission by one of the two speakers, who might cede "the floor" to another.

Both Peter and Steve were agreed on a philosophy of work and the evils of the machine—they followed the writings of the distributists of England and the Southern agrarians in this country. But Steve differed from Peter on works of mercy. He declaimed loudly with St. Paul, "He who does not work, neither let him eat." And no physical or mental disability won his pity. Men were either workers or shirkers. It was the conflict between the worker and scholar that Peter was always talking about. Steve considered himself both a worker and a scholar.

He did not attend church, but he used to say scornfully, when he was living with us on our hilltop farm near Easton, Pennsylvania, "If I believed as you do, that Christ Himself is present there on the altar, nothing in this world would keep me from it." He heard just enough of the discussion about the sacrament of duty and the self-imposed obligation of daily Mass and communion to know which side to take. He was a carper and constant critic, and sometimes his language was most immoderate. He aimed to goad, to irritate, and considered it the most effective agitation. Peter never irritated, but if Hergenhan became too vituperative he would walk away.

When he came to us, Peter begged him to consent to be used as a foil. Steve was to present the position of the Fascist, the totalitarian, and Peter was to refute him. They discoursed at our nightly meetings, in Union Square and Columbus Circle, and in Harlem, where we had been given the use of another store for the winter. They were invited to speak by Father Scully at a Holy Name meeting, and a gathering of the Knights of Columbus. How they loved these audiences in the simplicity of their hearts. Steve the German, Peter the Frenchman, both with strong accents, with oratory, with facial gesture, with striking pose, put on a show, and when they evoked laughter, they laughed too, delighted at amusing their audience, hoping to arouse them. "I am trying to make the encyclicals click," Peter used to say joyfully, radiant always before an audience. They never felt that they were laughed at. They thought they were being laughed with. Or perhaps they pretended not to see. They were men of poverty, of hard work, of Europe and America; they were men of vision; and they were men, too, with the simplicity of children.

But Hergenhan had bitterness too. The articles he wrote for *The Catholic Worker* about life in the Municipal Lodging

House and the quest for bread of the homeless were biting. After the first one appeared, one of the city officials drove up with some companions in a big car and with unctuous flattery praised the work we were doing and asked us why we did not come to them first rather than print such articles about the work of the city.

"I tried to tell you," Hergenhan said. "I tried to tell you of the graft, the poor food, the treatment we received, the contempt and kicking around we got. But you threatened me with the psychopathic ward. You treated me like a wild beast. You gave me the bum's rush."

Perhaps he looked to them like a dangerous radical, like a wild beast. In the helpless resentment of these men there was a fury which city authorities were afraid would gather into a flood of wrath, once they were gathered into a mob. So among every group in the public square, at the meetings of the unemployed, there were careful guardians of law and order watching, waiting to pounce on these gray men, the color of the lifeless trees and bushes and soil in the squares in winter, who had in them as yet none of the green of hope, the rising sap of faith.

Both Peter and Steve tried to arouse that hope. Both of them were personalists, both were workers. They did not want mass action, or violence. They were lambs in the simplicity of their program. They wanted to see the grass spring up between the cobbles of the city streets. They wanted to see the workers leave the cities with their wives and children and take to the fields, build themselves homes, where they would have room to breathe, to study, to pray, where there would be work for all.

"There is no unemployment on the land," Peter used to shout, and he would be met by jeers. "What about the migrants, the tenant farmers. They either work like slaves for the bosses, or they rot like the men in Tobacco Road."

"Fire the bosses," Peter used to say.

The trouble was that he never filled in the chasms, the valleys, in his leaping from crag to crag of noble thought.

He wanted men to think for themselves. Voluntary poverty, the doing without radios, cars, television sets, cigarettes, movies, cosmetics, all these luxuries, would enable men to buy the necessities. In a village community there would be work, even work in the gardens for the invalids, the children, the old, the crippled, the men and women who hung around the street corners and the marketplaces, waiting for someone to hire them.

"Personalism and communitarianism," was Peter's cry.

Steve wanted to flog men into action. His impatience was ferocious.

We were put out of the store in Harlem by the owner, who did not agree with our pacifism. As a member of the National Guard, he thought we were subversive. But not before there had been a riot in Harlem which wrecked store fronts, and resulted in some casualties to man and property. During the long night of the rioting, the Negroes who made up the mobs passed us by. "Don't touch this place," Steve and Peter and the old professor who inhabited the store heard them say. "These folks are all right," and the windows smashed all around them and the roaring of the mobs passed down the avenue. It was a fearful night, the men said, and it but reinforced their conviction of the futility of violence.

To build a new society within the shell of the old! It was the old I.W.W. slogan.

Soon we rented a twelve-room house with a big attic, in Huguenot, Staten Island, right on the water, and there Steve planted a garden which was a model to all who came to participate in week-end conferences. Groups of young people came, and speakers from Columbia University, from the Catholic University, from colleges in the Midwest, for these retreats and colloquiums. But as usual in groups working together, they went off on tangents and spent hours discussing rubrics and whether or not to say "compline" in English or Latin, and there was discussion too of machines and the land, organization and organism, the corporative order and the corporative state, and the rising tide of fascism and Nazism.

They all talked, and Steve talked with the best of them, but they were young and he was past fifty; they were young students, second- or third-generation Italian, German, French, Irish, and Peter and Steve were first generation. They listened to Peter because he never turned on them. Steve hated their avoidance of work, and after a good deal of recrimination turned from them to cultivate his garden.

The young fellows picketed the German consulate in protest against Nazism; they gave out literature at the docking of the *Bremen* and became involved in a riot when some Communists who called themselves Catholic workers tore down the swastika from the ship and were arrested. But Hergenhan just vented his scorn on youth in general and brought in great baskets of Swiss chard, tomatoes, beans, and squash for us to admire and eat. It choked him to see the young people eat them. He wanted disciples who would listen to him and work with him.

The next year we received a letter from a Baltimore schoolteacher who wished to invest in community. She offered us a thousand dollars provided we would build her a house and deed her three acres of the farm near Easton, Pennsylvania, to be purchased with her down payment. She would provide secondhand materials for the house.

We tried to dissuade her from coming to us, telling her of our dissensions, warning her she would be disappointed, but she insisted on contributing the money. She was disappointed, of course, but when she sold her little house some ten years later, she got out of it a great deal more than she put into it. That didn't prevent her from writing to the Archbishop of Baltimore telling him that she had been lured to contribute to our farming commune by promises of community, which promises had proved false.

Steve always insisted that he had built her house singlehanded. But Peter and John and Paul Cort helped clean secondhand brick, pull nails out of the secondhand lumber, cart water up the hill from the spring and cisterns, and dig the cellar, and there were many others who contributed many man-hours of labor. Of course much discussion went on with the building and digging. Hergenhan lived in a little shanty on the edge of the woods and came down to the farmhouse for his meals. He worked with great satisfaction on the house for two years. He was starting off the Catholic Workers with their first farming commune. He was showing them how to work, how to build, and he had great satisfaction in his toil. It was a spot of unutterable beauty looking down over the Delaware and the cultivated fields of New Jersey. Two and a half miles away at the foot of the hills were the twin cities of Easton and Philipsburg, one on either side of the river. Easton is a railroad center and a place of small factories, an old town with many historic buildings, and a college town, with Lafayette College perched upon a hill. There were Syrian, Lithuanian, German, Italian, and Irish churches, and we had all these nationalities among us, too.

Hergenhan built his house and then returned to the city to indoctrinate. He got tired of being considered the worker, and wanted to be a scholar for a time. But his bitterness had increased. In protest against our policies, specifically our works of mercy, he went to Camp La Guardia, a farm colony for homeless men run by the city. He wanted efficient and able-bodied workers building up village communities. We were clogged up with too much deadwood, with sluggish drones—it was the same old argument again, only this time it was a true worker and not just a young intellectual who was arguing the point.

He became ill and returned to us at Mott Street. We were his family after all. He was by then fifty-six. When he was examined the doctors discovered cancer, and after an operation he was taken to St. Rose's Cancer Hospital on the East Side, to die.

"Abandon hope all ye who enter here," he cried out when I came to visit him. He had not known of his cancer—they had talked of an intestinal obstruction at the hospital where the operation was performed—and when he was brought to St. Rose's he saw written over the door, *Home of the Cancerous Poor.*

His was a little room on the first floor; all day one could look into the garden and past that to the river where tugs and tankers steamed up and down the tidal river and clouds floated over the low shore of Brooklyn. The world was beautiful and he did not want to die. There was so much work he wanted to do, so small a part he had been allowed to play.

Peter and I used to go to see him every day. By that time I had just made what came to be known as our retreat and was filled with enthusiasm and ready to talk to anyone who would listen on the implications of the Christian life—and Steve always loved to converse, provided one gave him a chance to get in his share or the conversation.

I went to St. Rose's each day with my notes, and read them to him. He gradually became happy and reconciled. He had said, "There is so much I wanted to do." And I told him how Father John Hugo had talked of work, "that physical work was hard, mental work harder, and spiritual work was the hardest of all." And I pointed out that he was now doing the spiritual work of his life, lying there suffering, enduring, sowing all his own desires, in order to reap them in heaven. He began to realize that he had to die in order to live, that the door would open, that there was a glorious vista before him, "that all things were his."

"All things are yours," St. Paul wrote, "whether it be Paul or Apollo or Cephas, or the world, or life, or death, or things present, or things to come. For all are yours. And you are Christ's. And Christ is God's."

I read Bede Jarrett's *No Abiding City* to him, and some of Father Faber's conferences on death, and he enjoyed them all.

They offered him the richness of thought that he craved, and when the Sister who cared for him asked him if he did not want Baptism, he shouted wholeheartedly, "Yes!"

Peter and I were his sponsors, and to me it was a miracle of God's grace that the lack of dignity with which the Sacrament was conferred did not affront Steve, who was always hypercritical. He was baptized with speed and his confession listened to. He received Viaticum. I remember his anointing most vividly. Three other men were lined up on the bed at the same time, sitting there like gaunt old crows, their simple solemn faces lifted expectantly, childlike, watching every move of the priest, as he anointed their eyes, nose, mouth, ears, their claw-like hands stretched out to receive the holy oil, their feet with horny toes to which the priest bent with swift indifference.

He finished the job, he performed the outward signs, he recited the Latin prayers in a garbled monotone in the back of his throat, and despite the lack of grace in the human sense, Grace was there, souls were strengthened, hearts were lifted.

Ritual, how could we do without it! Though it may seem to be gibberish and irreverence, though the Mass is offered up in such haste that the sacred sentence "hoc est corpus meus" was abbreviated into "hocus-pocus" by the bitter protestor and has come down into our language meaning trickery, nevertheless there is a sureness and a conviction there. And just as a husband may embrace his wife casually as he leaves for work in the morning, and kiss her absent-mindedly in his comings and goings, still that kiss on occasion turns to rapture, a burning fire of tenderness and love. And with this to stay her she demands the "ritual" of affection shown. The little altar boy kissing the cruet of water as he hands it to the priest is performing a rite. We have too little ritual in our lives.

Steve was baptized and anointed but he did not rally. Daily he became weaker and weaker, and sometimes when I came I found him groaning with pain. Earlier at Roosevelt Hospital they had given him a brown-paper bag to blow into when he had an attack of pain. He would go through this ridiculous gesture as though he were going to break the bag explosively, as children do, but it was a desperate device like a woman's pulling on a roped sheet attached to the foot of the bed in the agonies of childbirth. Perhaps the intensity of pain and the intensity of pleasure are both somehow shameful because we so lose control, so lose ourselves, that we are no longer creatures of free will, but in the control of our blind flesh. "Who will deliver me from the body of this death?"

Steve died suddenly one morning, and there was no one with him. We found in his papers afterward notations which indicated his bitterness at not being more used, as writer, speaker, teacher. That has been the lament of so many who have died with us. Just as they are beginning to open their eyes to the glory and the potentialities of life their life is cut short as a weaver's thread. They were like the grass of the field. "The spaces of this life, set over against eternity, are most brief and poor," one of the desert Fathers said. It is part of the long loneliness.

There was the French professor who could speak many languages, and who was inventing a universal language. He had been a drug addict and had been cured. Now he had begun to drink, but it was only occasionally. He loved to go on nature walks, up along the Palisades and through Bear Mountain Park, with others who came together by correspondence. This was a part of his life we knew little about. He liked to translate articles for us, not for publication, but for our information. He would write them out in notebooks in a small fine hand, but when he gave them in, it was always with the expectation of money for something to drink. Since we passed many a day with little or no money on hand, and often had to run up gigantic grocery bills (our bill has gone as high as $6,000), he did not often get the fifty cents or a dollar he was expecting. Fifty cents was enough to start him off because he could buy a pint of wine on the Bowery for thirty-five cents.

One of our readers in Burlington, Vermont, a woman doctor who admired Peter Maurin very much, once told him that he could charge books to her account at Brentano's. For a while Peter had a field day. He was buying books for all his friends, even ordering them from England and from France. The professor found a way to increase his pay by asking Peter for dictionaries, German, Italian, French, Latin, Greek, et cetera. The friend in Burlington probably thought we were becoming impossibly intellectual, but she did not protest until bills came in for three French dictionaries. She wrote to us then saying that she could understand the need for one, but not for three. The professor had been selling them all. After that Peter limited his book-buying to one volume a week, and that for himself. It was a luxury, but also a necessity. It was the one luxury he enjoyed, and he shared it with young students who could not afford books and with others whom he tried to induce to read.

But as one young man who shared a room with Peter said, "Peter is always asking you to read his list of essential books, but when you settle down for a long evening of reading, he finds that an opportunity to talk." He liked catching you alone, serious and ready to think. He thought the role of teacher more effective than that of author.

There were these friends of Peter, some of them writing for the paper from the depths of their own experience. There were Margaret and Charlie and Francis who also wrote for the paper—Margaret, the Lithuanian girl, and Charlie, the convert Jew who used to sell gardenias on street corners, and Francis, who had been in Sing Sing for robbery with a Brooklyn gang. We knew many youths who had been in jail for robbery. The Italians love to gamble, and the stakes often reach into the thousands. Families have to mortgage homes, take up collections among themselves to pay off [the debt]. If other payment fails the youths are given "jobs" to do, and they find themselves part of a gang. They have seen the penalty for nonpayment of gambling debts in the slums in many a gang killing. One time, John Cort coming home from Mass saw a man lying dead in the center of the street, while the car from which the shooting was done sped away. John took the number of the license plates, though it was as much as his life was worth, but nothing ever came of this that we knew of. Women rushing out from tenements all around feared for their own. On this occasion, the young girl who lived in our house said to me bitterly, "There isn't a house on this block that hasn't got a son in Sing Sing."

Many college students and graduates came to live with us and to help us. It was usually the war or marriage which caused them to leave, or other opportunities for interesting work. But they always left with what they called their positions, their basic principles, firmly fixed in their minds, their faith confirmed, their lives in a way integrated. They did not go away to make a material success. And certainly there were many happy marriages. At *The Catholic Worker* there is always work for people to do. Peter glorified manual labor and taught what he liked to call his philosophy of labor. Ed Marciniak, one of the Chicago *Catholic Worker* group began a Labor weekly called *Work*. Ade Bethune wrote a pamphlet, *Work*, the size of a small book, which has run through many editions. Father Rembert Sorg, the Benedictine from St. Procopius Abbey in Chicago, had written a book called *Towards a Theology of Manual Labor* which has much in it from the early Fathers of the Church. This emphasis on the manual work of the world, which will go on no matter how many machines we may have to lighten labor, made students eager to help with hauling, cleaning, moving, cooking, and washing, all the multitude of household tasks that come up about a hospice.

In the early days, every afternoon saw visitors engaged in the work of moving evicted families. Now there are only occasional apartments for rent and occasional movings, but Helen Adler, one of the girls working with us, spent a number of months hunting apartments for women and children who were in the Municipal Lodging House. Charles McCormick, another of our staff, not only moved them but collected furniture from all over Greater New York, to supplement our own old furniture and also to help furnish the homes of the poor. He is kept busy driving to pick up food at the Essex Market, fish at the Fulton Market, or transporting supplies and our home-baked bread from our Staten Island farm to the city.

Selling the paper in front of Macy's or St. Francis' Church, or in Times Square or in front of Grand Central Station made one indeed look the fool. It was more natural to sell it along Fourteenth Street or Union Square where people were always selling or giving out literature. Once when we distributed along the waterfront to longshoremen, publicizing a meeting for longshoremen and seamen, one of them said, "They're always poking stuff at us, papers, posters, leaflets; first it's the Communists and then it's the Jehovah's Witnesses, and now it's the Catholics."

It was a difficult job, giving out literature, or selling the paper on the streets, but when one got used to it there was joy and freedom in it too, and the camaraderie of those who live on the streets and talk to each other freely. We learned their point of view. We were constantly confronted with the fact that on the one hand our daily papers, radio commentators, and now television were shaping the minds of the people, and yet they were still responsive to basic and simple religious truths. They were attached to the good; they were hardworking, struggling human beings living for the day, and afraid of the unknown.

Once that sense of fear of the unknown was overcome, brotherly love would evoke brother love, and mutual love would overcome fear and hatred.

The Communists recognized the power of the press, and also that the simple maxim "go to the people" meant literally going to them. The first time Trotsky was arrested it was for distributing literature at factory gates. When some of our friends were arrested in Chicago at stockyards during an organizational drive, we felt truly revolutionary and effective, since organized industry, through the hands of the law which they controlled, had reached out to stop us.

It is easy enough to write and publish a paper and mail it out with the help of volunteers to the four corners of the earth. But it becomes an actual, living thing when you get out on the street corners with the word, as St. Paul did in the early days of Christianity.

Labor

The Catholic Worker, as the name implied, was directed to the worker, but we used the word in its broadest sense, meaning those who worked with hand or brain, those who did physical, mental, or spiritual work. But we thought primarily of the poor, the dispossessed, the exploited.

Every one of us who was attracted to the poor had a sense of guilt, of responsibility, a feeling that in some way we were living on the labor of others. The fact that we were born in a certain environment, were enabled to go to school, were endowed with the ability to compete with others and hold our own, that we had few physical disabilities—all these things marked us as the privileged in a way. We felt a respect for the poor and destitute as those nearest to God, as those chosen by Christ for His compassion. Christ lived among men. The great mystery of the Incarnation, which meant that God became man that man might become God, was a joy that made us want to kiss the earth in worship, because His feet once trod that same earth. It was a mystery that we as Catholics accepted, but there were also the facts of Christ's life, that He was born in a stable, that He did not come to be a temporal

King, that He worked with His hands, spent the first years of His life in exile, and the rest of His early manhood in a crude carpenter shop in Nazareth. He fulfilled His religious duties in the synagogue and the temple. He trod the roads in His public life and the first men He called were fishermen, small owners of boats and nets. He was familiar with the migrant worker and the proletariat, and some of His parables dealt with them. He spoke of the living wage, not equal pay for equal work, in the parable of those who came at the first and the eleventh hour.

He died between two thieves because He would not be made an earthly King. He lived in an occupied country for thirty years without starting an underground movement or trying to get out from under a foreign power. His teaching transcended all the wisdom of the scribes and pharisees and taught us the most effective means of living in this world while preparing for the next. And He directed His sublime words to the poorest of the poor, to the people who thronged the towns and followed after John, the Baptist, who hung around, sick and poverty-stricken at the doors of rich men.

He had set us an example, and the poor and destitute were the ones we wished to reach. The poor were the ones who had jobs of a sort, organized or unorganized, and those who were unemployed or on work-relief projects. The destitute were the men and women who came to us in the breadlines, and we could do little with them but give what we had of food and clothing. Sin, sickness, and death accounted for much of human misery. But aside from this, we did not feel that Christ meant we should remain silent in the face of injustice and accept it even though He said, "The poor ye shall always have with you."

In the first issue of the paper we dealt with Negro labor on the levees in the South, exploited as cheap labor by the War Department. We wrote of women and children in industry and the spread of unemployment. The second issue carried a story of a farmers' strike in the Midwest and the condition of restaurant workers in cities. In the third issue there were stories of textile strikes and child labor in that industry; the next month coal and milk strikes. In the sixth issue of the paper we were already combating anti-Semitism. From then on, although we wanted to make our small eight-page tabloid a local paper, that is, covering the American scene, we could not ignore the issues abroad. They had their repercussions at home. We could not write about these issues without being drawn out on the streets on picket lines, and we found ourselves in 1935 with the Communists picketing the German consulate at the Battery.

It was not the first time we seemed to be collaborators. During the Ohrbach Department Store strike the year before I ran into old friends from the Communist group, but I felt then, and do now, that the fact that Communists made issue of Negro exploitation and labor trouble was no reason why we should stay out of the situation. "The truth is the truth," writes St. Thomas, "and proceeds from the Holy Ghost, no matter from whose lips it comes."

There was mass picketing every Saturday afternoon during the Ohrbach strike, and every Saturday the police drove up with patrol wagons and loaded the pickets into them with their banners and took them to jail. When we entered the dispute with our slogans drawn from the writings of the popes regarding the condition of labor, the police around Union Square were taken aback and did not know what to do. It was as though they were arresting the Holy Father himself, one of them said, were they to load our pickets and their signs into their patrol wagons. The police contented themselves with giving us all injunctions. One seminarian who stood on the side lines and cheered was given an injunction too, which he cherished as a souvenir.

Our readers helped us when they responded to our call not to trade with a store which paid poor wages and forced workers to labor long hours, and we helped defeat the injunction, one of the usual weapons used by employers to defeat picketing, which was handed down against the strikers. Now there is the Taft-Hartley law.

At that time one of the big Catholic high schools in the city each month received a bundle of three thousand copies of our paper for their students. I had spoken there of the work for the poor, and some of the students had worked with us. When we picketed the Mexican consulate to protest the religious persecution which was revived in 1934, the students came and joined us more than two thousand strong. We had set out, half a dozen of us, and, although we had printed an invitation in the paper, we did not expect such a hearty response. The police again were stunned at this demonstration, having met only with Communists in such mass demonstrations before. The students sang, marched, and rejoiced in the fact that their pictures appeared on the front page of the *Daily News* the next morning.

Among other readers who joined us that day was a young mate on a Standard Oil tanker who said he first read our paper while sailing in the Gulf. From then on he visited the office between trips and contributed half his salary to the work. Other picketers were Margaret, our cook, and her baby, and my daughter. Most belligerent was a young woman who had been sent to us from a hospital after an unsuccessful operation for [a] tumor on the brain. She was not too well informed as to issues and principles, and when one of the passers-by asked her what the picketing was about, she answered tartly, "None of your business."

She was one of those who liked to get out on the streets and sell the paper with Big Dan and a few others. There were many protests from the young intellectuals that these should seem to the public to represent the work. But they were certainly a part of it—"they belonged"—and they felt it and were fiercely loyal, though often they could make no answer for the faith that was in them.

The picketing of the Mexican consulate went well with the good Sisters who taught in a great Catholic high school, but when the students wanted to go on a picket line in a strike for the unionization of workers and better wages and hours, and were logical enough to extend their sympathy by boycotting the National Biscuit Company products and to inform their family grocers and delicatessens of this intention, then it was time for a stop. We were politely told that individuals could take the paper, but that the bundle order of three thousand must be canceled. There were too many people protesting against our activities with the students.

(On another occasion when I spoke to a high school group in Philadelphia, before I even returned to New York, a cancellation came in. "You must have done a good job down there," our circulation manager said grimly. "They used to take two thousand copies and now they've dropped them.")

Other readers who owned stock in N.B.C. sold their shares and informed the corporation. These acts helped settle the strike. The most spectacular help we gave in a strike was during the formation of the National Maritime Union. In May, 1936, the men appealed to us for help in housing and feeding some of the strikers, who came off the ships with Joe Curran in a spontaneous strike against not only the shipowners but also the old union leaders.

We had then just moved St. Joseph's house to 115 Mott Street and felt that we had plenty of room. Everyone camped out for a time while seamen occupied the rooms which they made into dormitories. There were about fifty of them altogether during the course of the next month or so, and a number of them became friends of the work.

There were O'Toole, a cook on the United States Lines, and Mike, a Portuguese engineer who carried copies of *The Catholic Worker* to Spain when he shipped out later, bringing us back copies of papers and magazines from Barcelona. This same friend brought us a bag full of earth from Mount Carmel after his ship had touched at the Holy Land. Once he asked me what I wanted from India, and I told him the kind of a spindle which Gandhi had sent to Chiang Kai-shek, as a gift and a warning, perhaps against United States industrialism. He and a shipmate searched in several Indian ports for what I wanted and finally found three spindles in Karachi, which they brought to me. One was a metal hand spinner shaped like those shown in old pictures which could be carried about in a little box; the other two were most peculiar contraptions, one of them looking like a portable phonograph.

The seamen came and went and most of them we never saw again, but three remained for years and joined in our work. That first strike was called off, but in the fall, after the men built up their organization, the strike call went out again. For the duration of the strike we rented a store on Tenth Avenue and used it as a reading room and soup kitchen where no soup was served, but coffee and peanut butter and apple butter sandwiches. The men came in from picket lines and helped themselves to what they needed. They read, they talked, and they had time to think. Charlie O'Rourke, John Cort, Bill Callahan, and a number of seamen kept the place open all day and most of the night. There was never any disorder; there were no maneuverings, no caucuses, no seeking of influence or power; it was simply a gesture of help, the disinterested help of brothers, inspired in great part by our tanker friend, Jim McGovern, who had written an article for the paper telling how he had been treated as a seaman in Russia and the kind of treatment these same men got here.

Jim was a college graduate, had fallen away from his early faith, but regained it by reading Claudel. He was so painfully shy that he was no good at all in contacts with the rank and file. He went to sea because he loved it; he loved the ship he served and the responsibility it entailed. Perhaps there was much of romance and youth in his attitude. He wrote to us of the clubs in the Russian port, and how the men were treated as men, capable of appreciating lectures, concerts, dances, and meetings with student groups. In this country, he said, the seamen were treated as the scum of the earth; port towns and the port districts in these towns were slums and water-front streets made up of taverns and pawnshops and houses of prostitution. He felt that the Russians treated their American comrades as though they were creatures of body and soul, made in the image and likeness of God (though atheism was an integral part of Marxism), and here in our professedly Christian country they were treated like beasts, and often became beasts because of this attitude.

Our headquarters were a tribute to the seaman's dignity as a man free to form association with his fellows, to have some share in the management of the enterprise in which he was engaged.

On another occasion, when the Borden Milk Company attempted to force a company union on their workers, *The Catholic Worker* took up their cause, called public attention to the use of gangsters and thugs to intimidate the drivers, and urged our readers to boycott the company's products while unfair conditions prevailed. As a result of the story the company attacked *The Catholic Worker* in paid advertisements in the Brooklyn *Tablet* and the *Catholic News*.

Many times we have been asked why we spoke of *Catholic* workers, and so named the paper. Of course it was not only because we who were in charge of the work, who edited the paper, were all Catholics, but also because we wished to influence Catholics. They were our own, and we reacted sharply to the accusation that when it came to private morality the Catholics shone but when it came to social and political morality, they were often conscienceless. Also Catholics were the poor, and most of them had little ambition or hope of bettering their condition to the extent of achieving ownership of home or business or further education for their children. They accepted things as they were with humility and looked for a better life to come. They thought, in other words, that God meant it to be so.

At the beginning of the organizing drive of the Committee (now the Congress) for Industrial Organization, I went to Pittsburgh to write about the work in the steel districts. Mary

Heaton Vorse was there at the time, and we stayed at Hotel
Pitt together in the cheapest room available, at a dollar and
a half a day. It was before we had the house of hospitality in
Pittsburgh which now stands on the top of a hill in the Negro
district. A student reader of the paper drove us around to all
the little towns, talking of his soul, much to Mary's distress;
she was especially distracted when he told of practicing pen-
ances on our Easton farm by going out at night and rolling
in some brambles. He had no interest in the struggles of the
workers—it was the spiritual side of our work which appealed
to him—and he was driving us through all the complicated
districts on either side of rivers not so much to help us, as to
help himself. He wanted to talk to us about his problems.
There was not the quiet and peace on such trips to make such
talk very fruitful.

There had been the big strike in 1919 led by William Z.
Foster, which Mary had covered, and she knew some of the
old priests who had helped the people by turning the base-
ments of their churches into relief centers. We went to see
them, and we attended open-air meetings along the Monon-
gahela and the Allegheny and Ohio rivers, where we distributed papers.

On that visit Bishop Hugh Boyle said to me, "You can go
into all the parishes in the diocese with my blessing, but half
the pastors will throw you out." He meant that they did not
have that social consciousness which I was seeking among
Catholics and that they felt all organizations of workers were
dominated by Communists and were a danger to be avoided.

Later in the big steel strikes in Chicago and Cleveland,
when "Little Steel" fought it out with the workers, there was
tragedy on the picket lines. In what came to be called the
Memorial Day massacre, police shot down hundreds out on
the prairies in front of the Republic Steel plants in South
Chicago. Ten men died, and others were disabled for life. I
had just visited their soup kitchens and strike headquarters;
in addition to recognizing that the majority of the workers

were Catholics, I also recognized an old friend, Elizabeth, the wife of Jack Johnstone, one of the Communist party leaders in this country. Elizabeth and Jack had brought me roast chicken and ginger ale one night as I lay sick with influenza in New York, and Elizabeth had taken care of Tamar for me so that I could go to Mass, and I had taken care of her young son. Elizabeth, whom I had last seen in New York, was there to write a pamphlet on "Women in Steel," a call to the wives and mothers to help their men organize. Her husband had been organizing in India, and they were accustomed to long separations during which both of them worked for the party. Elizabeth used to tease me by saying that it was due to me that she had become a member of the party and had met Jack, because I had obtained a job for her with the Anti-Imperialist League, where I was working at the time.

Elizabeth in Chicago, Jack in India—these wives of Communists, dedicated to revolution as Rayna was! Rayna's husband had worked in the Philippines while she was in Hankow. They went where they were sent, had a sense of their world mission, and accepted any hardship that it entailed. If I could only arouse Catholics to such zeal, with the spiritual weapons at their disposal, I thought! If they could only be induced to accept voluntary poverty as a principle, so that they would not fear the risk of losing job, of losing life itself. Organizing sometimes meant just that.

It was not only the Communists, however, who had this courage. One winter I had a speaking engagement in Kansas and my expenses were paid, which fact enabled me to go to Memphis and Arkansas to visit the Tenant Farmers' Union, which was then and is still headed by a Christian Socialist group. The headquarters were a few rooms in Memphis, where the organizers often slept on the floor because there was no money for rent other than that of the offices. Those days I spent with them I lived on sandwiches and coffee because there was no money to spend on regular meals either. We needed to save money for gas to take us around to the centers where dispossessed sharecroppers and tenant farmers were also camping out, homeless, in railroad stations, schools, and churches. They were being evicted wholesale because of the purchase of huge tracts of land by northern insurance agencies. The picture has been shown in *Tobacco Road*, *In Dubious Battle*, and *Grapes of Wrath*—pictures of such desolation and poverty and in the latter case of such courage that my heart was lifted again to hope and love and admiration that human beings could endure so much and yet have courage to go on and keep their vision of a more human life.

During that trip I saw men, women, and children herded into little churches and wayside stations, camped out in tents, their household goods heaped about them, not one settlement but many—farmers with no land to farm, housewives with no homes. They tried with desperate hope to hold onto a pig or some chickens, bags of seed, some little beginnings of a new hold on life. It was a bitter winter and frame houses there are not built to withstand the cold as they are in the north. The people just endure it because the winter is short—accept it as part of the suffering of life.

I saw children ill, one old man dead in bed and not yet buried, mothers weeping with hunger and cold. I saw bullet holes in the frame churches, and their benches and pulpit smashed up and windows broken. Men had been kidnapped and beaten; men had been shot and wounded. The month after I left, one of the organizers was killed by a member of a masked band of vigilantes who were fighting the Tenant Farmers' Union.

There was so little one could do—empty one's pockets, give what one had, live on sandwiches with the organizers, and write, write to arouse the public conscience. I telegraphed Eleanor Roosevelt and she responded at once with an appeal to the governor for an investigation. The papers were full of the effrontery of a northern Catholic social worker, as they called me, who dared to pay a four-day visit and pass judgment on the economic situation of the state. The governor visited some of the encampments, and sarcastic remarks were made in some of the newspaper accounts about the pigs and chickens. "If they are starving, let them eat their stock," they wrote.

I spoke to meetings of the unemployed in California, to migrant workers, tenant farmers, steelworkers, stockyard workers, auto workers. The factory workers were the aristocrats of labor. Yet what a struggle they had!

There was that migrant worker I picked up when I drove in a borrowed car down through the long valley in California, writing about government aid to the agricultural workers. "Nothing I love so much as jest to get out in a field and chop cotton," he said wistfully.

There was that old Negro living in a little shack in Alabama where the rain fell through on the rags that covered him at night. While I talked to him a little boy ran up and gave him a bone and some pieces of corn-bread; the old man was so excited talking to me and the priest who was with me that he dropped the bone on the ground and a hound dog started licking it. The little boy stood by him, pulling at his sleeve and crying. It was his dinner too, his only dinner, and it was being devoured by a dog. If the old man had more, the children would have less. And there was so little.

There was that little girl in Harrisburg, and another in Detroit, sent out by their parents to prostitute themselves on the street. While I talked to the family in Harrisburg, all of whom lived in one room, the little girl sat reading a tattered book, *Dorothy Vernon of Haddon Hall.*

There was Paul St. Marie, who was president of the first Ford local, a tool and die maker, with a wife and eight children. He suffered from unemployment, from discrimination when he was hired. He worked the graveyard shift from twelve to eight, walked a mile from gate to plant, and worked in the cold on stone floors. He fell ill with rheumatic fever at the age of forty-five and died. He knew poverty and insecurity and living on relief—he and his wife were heroic figures in the labor movement, thinking of their fellows more than of themselves. Paul took me around the auto plants and showed me what the assembly line meant. I met the men who were beaten to a pulp when they tried to distribute literature at plant gates, and I saw the unemployed who had fire hoses turned on them during an icy winter when they hung around the gates of the Ford plant looking for work.

"How close are you to the worker?" Pitirim Sorokin asked me when I was talking with him at Harvard. He himself was the son of a peasant woman and a migrant worker and was imprisoned three times under the Czars and three times under the Soviets. He too had suffered exile in the forests, hunger, and imprisonment; he had lived under the sentence of death and was, through some miracle, and probably because of his doctrine of love in human behavior, allowed to go abroad. He had a right to ask such a question and it was a pertinent one.

Going around and seeing such sights is not enough. To help the organizers, to give what you have for relief, to pledge yourself to voluntary poverty for life so that you can share with your brothers is not enough. One must live with them, share with them their suffering too. Give up one's privacy, and mental and spiritual comforts as well as physical.

Our Detroit house of hospitality for women is named for St. Martha. We are always taking care of migrant families in that house, southern families who are lured to the North because they hear of the high wages paid. It is a house of eight large rooms, and each of the bedrooms has housed a family with children, but the congestion has meant that the husbands had to go to the men's house of hospitality named for St. Francis. Sometimes the families overflow into a front parlor and living room downstairs. The colored take care of the white children, and the white the colored, while the parents hunt for homes and jobs. Such an extreme of destitution makes all men brothers.

Yes, we have lived with the poor, with the workers, and we know them not just from the streets, or in mass meetings, but from years of living in the slums, in tenements, in our hospices in Washington, Baltimore, Philadelphia, Harrisburg, Pittsburgh, New York, Rochester, Boston, Worcester, Buffalo, Troy, Detroit, Cleveland, Toledo, Akron, St. Louis, Chicago, Milwaukee, Minneapolis, Seattle, San Francisco, Los Angeles, Oakland, even down into Houma, Louisiana where Father Jerome Drolet worked with Negroes and whites, with shrimp shellers, fishermen, longshoremen, and seamen.

Just as the Church has gone out through its missionaries into the most obscure towns and villages, we have gone too. Sometimes our contacts have been through the Church and sometimes through readers of our paper, through union organizers or those who needed to be organized.

We have lived with the unemployed, the sick, the unemployables. The contrast between the worker who is organized and has his union, the fellowship of his own trade to give him strength, and those who have no organization and come in to us on a breadline is pitiable.

They are stripped then, not only of all earthly goods, but of spiritual goods, their sense of human dignity. When they are forced into line at municipal lodging houses, in clinics, in our houses of hospitality, they are then the truly destitute. Over and over again in our work, many young men and women who come as volunteers have not been able to endure it and have gone away. To think that we are forced by our own lack of room, our lack of funds, to perpetuate this shame, is heartbreaking.

"Is this what you meant by houses of hospitality," I asked Peter.

"At least it will arouse the conscience," he said.

Many left the work because they could see no use in this gesture of feeding the poor, and because of their own shame. But enduring this shame is part of our penance.

"All men are brothers." How often we hear this refrain, the rallying call that strikes a response in every human heart. These are the words of Christ, "Call no man master, for ye are all brothers." It is a revolutionary call which has even been put to music. The last movement of Beethoven's Ninth Symphony has that great refrain—"All men are brothers." Going to the people is the purest and best act in Christian tradition and revolutionary tradition and is the beginning of world brotherhood.

Never to be severed from the people, to set out always from the point of view of serving the people, not serving the interests of a small group or oneself. "To believe in the infinite creative power of the people," Mao Tse-tung, the secretary of the Communist party in China, wrote with religious fervor. And he said again in 1943, "The maxim 'three common men will make a genius' tells us that there is great creative power among the people and that there are thousands and thousands of geniuses among them. There are geniuses in every village, every city." It is almost another way of saying that we must and will find Christ in each and every man, when we look on them as brothers.

At a group meeting in New York, part of the Third Hour movement, made up of Catholics, Russian Orthodox, and Protestants of all denominations, a Socialist said to me that the gesture of going to the people was futile and that it had been tried in Russia and failed. We had a long discussion on the validity of such efforts to achieve brotherhood, and I kept repeating that the Christian point of view was to keep in mind the failure of the Cross. Then thinking I might be talking to someone with a Jewish background, I spoke of the natural order itself, how the seed must fall into the ground and die in order to bear fruit. In the labor movement every strike is considered a failure, a loss of wages and man power, and no one is ever convinced that understanding between employer and worker is any clearer or that gains have been made on either side; and yet in the long history of labor, certainly there has been a slow and steady bettering of conditions. Women no longer go down into the mines, little children are not fed into the mills. In the long view the efforts of the workers have achieved much.

At the close of the evening, I learned that I had been talking to Alexander Kerensky, one of the greatest failures in history.

My trips around the country were usually to visit our houses of hospitality, which were springing up everywhere, and also to speak at schools. I took advantage of these trips to cover strikes and the new organizational drive of the Congress of Industrial Organizations.

Father James G. Keller, head of the Christopher Movement, called me one day and said that Archbishop McNicholas would like to talk to me, so I took a train to Cincinnati. Usually I travel by bus in order to economize. But this time the Archbishop sent a ticket and I traveled comfortably. I spent the day with him and with several other bishops of the Midwest, discussing the condition of the unemployed and the strikes that were going on in the auto plants. We were served magnificently at the bishops' table but the Archbishop himself dined modestly on a few vegetables and milk. I could not help thinking, of course, of our breadlines, and our cramped quarters. It is not only the Archbishop's palace which is a contrast, but every rectory in our big cities, and even in country sections. Only in the mission fields is the rectory as poor as the homes of the workers round about. One can understand the idea of a functional society and the needs of doctors for cars and telephones and of the lawyer and teacher for books and space, but the ordinary family has need of space too for his little church which is his family.

For Christ Himself, housed in the tabernacles in the Church no magnificence is too great, but for the priest who serves Christ, and for the priesthood of the laity, no such magnificence, in the face of the hunger and homelessness of the world, can be understood.

And yet I do know too that if any bishop or archbishop started to take the poor into his palace, or moved out of his palace to live with the poor, he would be considered mad. And he would suffer the fate of the fool.

Bishops and priests may long to make that gesture, but their own humility no doubt restrains them. Some day may God put His hand upon them so unmistakably that they know they are called to this gesture, to this madness. We begin to see a little of it in Archbishop Stepinac, who told C. L. Sulzberger of the *New York Times* that he would not be other than where he was, in a prison cell, doing penance for the Church.

"The Church is the Cross on which Christ was crucified, and who can separate Christ from His Cross," Guardini has written.

On that happy occasion when I enjoyed the day with the Archbishop, who, like so many others, lived in poverty in the midst of wealth, Father Keller and I listened to him read a pastoral letter he had just written. It was about the condition of capital and labor, and I felt it was a noble piece of writing. But Father Keller thought the Archbishop was a trifle harsh to the rich.

That night when I discussed going to Detroit to cover the situation of the sit-down strikers in the Flint auto plants, the Archbishop urged me to go to them, to write about them. He had one of his priests reserve and pay for a Pullman berth for me so that I would be fresh the next day for my work.

It was a friendly and a happy day of talk about the needs of the workers and the poor. It made me unhappy later when the Archbishop became so uneasy about *The Catholic Worker*'s editorial position on the Spanish Civil War that he asked pastors in his diocese to discontinue getting it for their churches or schools, though he did not suggest that they cease taking it themselves.

On another occasion he issued a call in one of his public statements, for a mighty army of conscientious objectors if we embarked upon a war with Russia as an ally. Those of our associates around the country who swelled the ranks of the Catholic conscientious objectors looked ruefully on the anything-but-mighty army. They also felt that they were conscientious objectors for the same reason that they opposed the war in Spain, or class war or race war or imperialist war, not because Russia was our ally.

The Archbishop gave us three hundred dollars as a contribution toward our camp for conscientious objectors, and we deeply appreciated this first gesture of ecclesiastical friendship in our hitherto unheard-of position. Before he died he sent us his blessing again.

But I am trying to write about the bishops in connection with the labor movement. Archbishop Schrembs of Cleveland was always friendly when I visited him at those times I was invited to speak at congress and social-action meetings. I visited strike headquarters during the Little Steel strike and talked with the men. They were worn with the protracted conflict and worried about losing the homes they had managed to buy after years of saving, and the food and clothing needed for their children if they lost both strike and job as had happened on other occasions in the past. The next day when I visited Archbishop Schrembs he told me that during the morning a representative of Associated Industries had called on him and told him of my presence at strike headquarters the day before.

In New York the Chancery office had also been informed of our activities, and when a priest came to see us in our Tenth Avenue headquarters during the seamen's strike the visit was immediately reported. This happened often enough to indicate to me that there were spies from the employers among the strikers and that the employers felt that the Church was on their side in any industrial dispute. The worker present at Mass was in the eyes of bishop and priest just like any member of Knights of Columbus or Holy Name Society, but as soon as he went on strike he became a dangerous radical, and the publicity he got linked him with saboteurs and Communists.

We met other bishops who visited our offices and told us about the work in their dioceses, in the co-operative movement, parish credit unions, circulating libraries and other activities among the laity. They sat down to eat with us—Bishop O'Hara, Bishop Waters, Bishop Busch—and abbots of monasteries, who are also princes of the Church, came too. Every six months when we sent out our appeals, there were a number of bishops who always responded, even those who disagreed so strongly on some aspects of our work that they would not permit meetings in their dioceses and certainly not houses of hospitality. However, some houses opened up not specifically associated with *The Catholic Worker*, but owing their inspiration to it. Those who run these houses feel themselves to be children of the movement since they work with the poor and dispossessed. However, they do not hold to the distributist or anarchist or pacifist positions that are taken editorially in *The Catholic Worker*. They leave the discussion of these issues to others, and do the immediate work of showing their love for their brothers in the simple practical method of the corporal works of mercy.

The spiritual works of mercy include enlightening the ignorant, rebuking the sinner, consoling the afflicted, as well as bearing wrongs patiently, and we have always classed picket lines and the distribution of literature among these works.

During the course of writing about labor and capital, we began a study club at the Mott Street headquarters. It was an outgrowth of the seamen's strike and was started by John Cort, a young Harvard graduate who was working with us at the time, and Martin Wersing, a union official in the electrical workers. Father John Monaghan and a group of other union men joined with them in forming what they called the Association of Catholic Trade Unionists. After it had obtained its start under our auspices, the group moved to Canal Street so that they would have room for their meetings and could handle the avalanche of inquiry which came to them, once they were under way.

Their aim and endeavor were to assist the worker to organize and to enlighten the Catholic in the existing unions as to the teachings of the popes in regard to labor. They set out at once to oppose the Communist and gangster elements (two separate problems) in the longshoreman and other unions, and their policy came into conflict with ours.

As Peter pointed out, ours was a long-range program, looking for ownership by the workers of the means of production, the abolition of the assembly line, decentralized factories, the restoration of crafts and ownership of property. This meant, of course, an accent on the agrarian and rural aspects of our economy and a changing of emphasis from the city to the land.

The immediate job at hand was enough for the Association. They disagreed too with our indiscriminate help in strikes where there was strong Communist influence, and our loss of the opportunity to get our own men into positions of vantage in order to influence others.

Peter, however, talked about Christ's technique, of working from the bottom and with the few, of self-discipline and self-organization, of sacrifice rather than enlightened self-interest, and of course, of the synthesis of cult, culture, and cultivation. How he loved the roll of that phrase. Once when he spoke to the seamen at the Tenth Avenue strike headquarters he attacked communism, but it was by reviewing a book by Andre Gide and by talking of his disillusionment with the Russian regime. I supposed he considered the meeting from the standpoint of culture, most of the seamen never having heard of Andre Gide, or if they had, only of the unsavory aspects of his erotic life. Sometimes we used to sigh over Peter's idea as to what would be dynamic thought for the workers.

There is so much more to the Catholic Worker Movement than labor and capital. It is people who are important, not the masses. When I read Pope Pius XII's Christmas message, in which he distinguished between the masses and the people, I almost wished I had named our publication *The People*, instead of *The Catholic Worker*.

We published many heavy articles on capital and labor, on strikes and labor conditions, on the assembly line and all the other evils of industrialism. But it was a whole picture we were presenting of man and his destiny and so we emphasized less, as the years went by, the organized-labor aspect of the paper.

It has been said that it was *The Catholic Worker* and its stories of poverty and exploitation that aroused the priests to start labor schools, go out on picket lines, take sides in strikes with the worker, and that brought about an emphasis on the need to study sociology in the seminaries.

And many a priest who afterward became famous for his interest in labor felt that we had in a way deserted the field, had left the cause of the union man. Bishops and priests appearing on the platforms of the A. F. of L. and C.I.O. conventions felt that we had departed from our original intention and undertaken work in the philosophical and theological fields that might better have been left to the clergy. The discussion of the morality of modern war, for instance, and application of moral principle in specific conflicts. Labor leaders themselves felt that in our judgment of war, we judged them also for working in the gigantic armaments race, as indeed we did. Ours is indeed an unpopular front.

When we began our work there were thirteen million unemployed. The greatest problem of the day was the problem of work and the machine.

The state entered in to solve these problems by dole and work relief, by setting up so many bureaus that we were swamped with initials. NIRA gave the plan to NRA, and as NRA was declared unconstitutional another organization, another administration was set up. The problem of the modern state loomed up as never before in American life. The Communists, stealing our American thunder, clamored on the one hand for relief and on the other set up Jeffersonian schools of democracy.

Peter also quoted Jefferson—"He governs best who governs least." One of his criticisms of labor was that it was aiding in the creation of the Welfare State, the Servile State, instead of aiming for the ownership of the means of production and acceptance of the responsibility that it entailed.

III

Socially Engaged Spirituality

This reflection on the spirituality represented in the work of Walter Rauschenbusch and Dorothy Day aims at examining the foundations of a socially engaged Christian life. But the large perspective on what they share in common should not blur the distinctiveness of these writers: they were very different. The contrast is in the distinct periods of American history. Rauschenbusch was a social historian and an academic after being a pastor, and Day left the university to become a journalist. He was an analytical theologian, she was practical and efficient. He was didactic, she bore witness. One was liberal and progressive, the other a radical anarchist. Behind the differences, however, lay digested spheres of social meaning that in fact were complementary. Both represent a positive, constructive spirituality of resistance to social injustice. They did not dwell on personal moral blame or guilt but appealed to all by addressing what could be done by all collectively, at least on the level of common commitment. Their universal appeal did not lie in specific programs and actions, because each was responding to a broad crisis in a particular way. But like no other time in the history of Christian spirituality, they both center their attention on social justice.[1] They represent an orientation that seeks dedication to a common cause but leaves open different ways of understanding and achieving it. Drawing constructively from both as complementary sources, the five following insights remain relevant and crucial for our own time, *mutatis mutandis*.

Distinct Spiritualities of Social Engagement

The contrast between these two writers correlates with the distinct style of spirituality that each represents. Examining the contrast aims less at establishing types than simply noticing different ways Christian spirituality can engage society; a shared historical situation always generates particulars that are different and authors who are unique. One has to be careful in contrasting these spiritualities lest the descriptions appear to be offered in a competitive way. There is no zero-sum relationship here, as if something stressed by one would appear neglected by the other. Where one appears more, the other would not necessarily be less but may simply be situated differently. The analysis shows that history shapes freedom and encourages creative adaptation. Only after trying to adjust spirituality to the situation do we need to dwell on the distinctiveness that ensures its realism and authenticity.

Is there a formula that captures Rauschenbusch's spirituality in a way that shows its relevance for our time? Although he welcomed the idea of "Christianizing society," a clearer consciousness of religious pluralism today underlines the fact that, because the United States can have no established religion, it cannot be a Christian nation. But a softer, less literal understanding of the phrase avoids a naïve understanding of Rauschenbusch's mission. His intent was to make Christian self-understanding and values, wherever they exist, including the social structures that are sustained in place without reflection on their implications, relevant to the whole of life.

The sentiment is analogously transferrable to other faith traditions. He did not intend to reestablish the ecclesiastical authority of a pre-Enlightened Western world, but to overcome a narrowing inward turn after the Enlightenment. The generative impulse of Rauschenbusch's spirituality can be found in the way he re-educated himself as a pastor and sought to draw out the social, political, and economic relevance of being and acting like a Christian in a time that needed public Christian values. Rauschenbusch's spirituality makes no sense as either Christian supremacism or as social utopianism. It responds to the simple critical question of what Christian faith says about being a good citizen in a structurally unjust society.

Two dimensions to Rauschenbusch's spirituality bear special attention: he wants to find God within the world and make clear where God's values come to bear upon it. A theme that unites both writers can be stated as "finding God within the world" of social relationships. Rauschenbusch stresses that one encounters God by responding to the social situation that is causing so much suffering. He recognizes that the response has to be different than the Christian charity of the past. A battle between unjust social structures and philanthropy makes no sense. Social justice has to do with the institutions and the social patterns of behavior that deliver social injury. Rauschenbusch's social consciousness was such that he and other social Christians thought in terms of structures and systems. Social misery cannot be ameliorated by leaving in place the systems that cause the injustice and dealing with individuals and groups by charity or the dole. The Christian should seek instead to implement God's will by addressing the structures of oppression. The immediate goal is not to convert the world to Christianity, but to make Christians responsible for the world. The plea, "Thy Kingdom come!" was a call for human agents. In his words, corporate Christian spirituality would be "organized around Jesus Christ as its impelling power, and would have for its sole or chief object to embody his spirit in its life and to carry him into human thought and the conduct of affairs."[2]

The distinctiveness of Dorothy Day's spirituality readily appears in the contrast with Rauschenbusch. She does not directly appeal to the intellectuals and leaders of society with transformative ideas and programs, but to those who would care for the victims of society. Her spirituality is one of accompaniment, of embodiment of the direct ministry of Jesus to those who suffer, and of witness to the deeper values of human existence by care for individuals.[3] Beneath the ministry of accompaniment, its foundation, lies the bedrock of personalism. "There is so much more to the Catholic Worker Movement than labor and capital. It is people who are important, not the masses."[4] Whether the personalism led her back to God, or whether God appeared as the ground of the dignity and value of the human person, this conviction grounds her vision.[5]

She envisions a society that values human life, but her spirituality is less analytical and strategic and more an institutionalized programmatic public witness. Its force lies in its radicality, giving it power analogous to the spirit of Francis of Assisi. Her statement is extreme. One can draw analogies between the foundations of monasticism in its context and the basic witness born by the Worker movement in a new environment. Day's spirituality of accompaniment demanded in some ways a more radical commitment to identify with the poor and to work with the poor and other marginalized groups. But, as in monasticism, a deep correlation bordering on identity unites the institutional structure of the Worker movement and the spirituality of the people who do this work of accompaniment; the movement embodies their spirituality.

A New Set of Intellectual Presuppositions

Both Walter Rauschenbusch and Dorothy Day were drawn into a new set of intellectual presuppositions for understanding the social political world. This sweeping statement needs more justification and nuance than is given here, but even as a hypothesis it illumines their thought and its reception. Historical and social consciousness were fundamentally altered with Marx's critical sociology of knowledge. He introduced ideas frequently taken for granted today. Social place and time condition our opinions and our knowledge. Moreover, reflection on the social constitution of thought engenders a new sense of responsibility for the structures of society that are in place and the character of our convictions. Against an implicit individualism of being and perception that is encouraged by a fatalistic view of society, these new suppositions open up possibilities of change and stimulate new initiatives. They call into question an enlightened bias toward a universally relevant knowledge of things; all our views are related to their historical social context and other vectors of influence: gender, race or culture, genetic make-up, education, talents, and so on. As enlightened thought challenged authority, social historical consciousness challenged enlightened social and economic structures with a new sense of corporate responsibility.

These ideas were not organized into a neat package and were not available for observation. Both Rauschenbusch and Day had to be converted to this many-faceted perspective. The conversion of Rauschenbusch was negotiated through the impact that the conditions in which the people in his church were living had on every aspect of their lives. This drew him into the critical social discussion that was whirling around in social, political, economic, philosophical, and then theological circles. The conversion of Dorothy Day took a much longer time; it began with her questions about society in a university setting and continued until Peter Maurin offered her a response which was not a resolution but an intentional plan of a way to live. Both stories indicate that social-historical consciousness has to be learned and internalized; it is not overtly available but requires reflection and inference.

Beneath both experiences lies a negative experience of contrast, in this case a large negative phenomenon, that first forces the mind to take cognizance and figure it out. Then, secondly, once it takes hold, it acts like a new framework or horizon that rearranges all the furniture of the mind.

Change in Theological Perspective

Both Rauschenbusch and Day represent a shift in perspective on the relation between persons and society. This change need not be considered in the aggressive terms of an either/or. A new perspective may preserve traditional doctrines while allowing them to take on fuller, more extensive, and relevant meaning. These writings illustrate a change in perspective on views of human existence from one that begins with the individual human person to one that focuses on human existence as a collectivity and sees individuals as members.

These two points of view make a difference in theological understanding. When doctrines deal with God as God relates to human beings, it matters whether the human being referred to is I, as an individual, or all human beings in more general terms and as policy. Christian doctrine holds that God relates to all people equally, and this direct relationship grounds the value of each one. At the same time, human beings are members of communities, and one cannot think of one's personal relation to God as outside the sphere of the community. These distinct perspectives and how they related to each other developed in the course of the Enlightenment and the nineteenth century. The authority of the churches was greatly reduced or even separated from the political and economic spheres of secular society. This resulted in a tendency to restrict the meaning of the Christian message to the private sphere of the individual or the religious group.[6] Gradually Christian authority and the sphere of spiritual responsibility lost some or much of their social relevance and their bearing on the political and social spheres.[7]

The examples of sin, grace, and salvation provide good "places" where one can fairly easily appreciate the expansion and contraction of meaning that accompanies theological reflection. The social gospel represents an opening up of the framework that guides one's thinking about these spiritual realities. Rauschenbusch and Day reflected extensively on questions about evil and sin: Why is there so much innocent social suffering in the world? Where does responsibility lie, if it does not lie with God? It is far from obvious that one can describe the radical negativity of the social degradation of human life as sin. When one does call it sin, however, it calls up the corporate responsibility for the situation that engages both the leaders and the people of a democracy. One cannot call upon fate, because some societies do better than others in dealing with social suffering. The idea of "sin" reminds us that as participants we share some collective responsibility for the situation.

A notion of corporate sin also expands the meaning of grace and salvation when it includes the gracious dimensions of everyday life that make it blessing rather than torture. Social sin empowers spirituality by a spontaneous reaction against its effects. Corporate human suffering stimulates a desire to resist it. It is crucial, however, to understand that neither Rauschenbusch nor Day proposes a social historical way of thinking that cancels the personalism characteristic of the private individual sphere. Social consciousness does not restrict but expands understanding of the human person. Neither Rauschenbusch nor Day can be associated with re-ductionism. They both nurtured a strong personalism in their ministries and in their formulations of a social gospel spiri-tuality. In fact, the social gospel appeals to personal reflection and decision; it encourages the internal freedom of a person to transcend the social self.

Rauschenbusch provides a good example of how a change in one's social perspective influences an understanding of doctrine and spirituality. It is natural enough to think of re-ligious experience and faith in individual personalist terms.

One's basic spirituality, first of all, seems to be grounded in personal attachment to God: God's address to a person and his or her response form the elementary core of salvation. Salvation has a decisively primal sense in the personal onto-logical terms of union with God. In a second spontaneous overflow of this attachment, one loves the neighbor. Luther's spirituality of gratitude illustrates this well. Just as society is made up of individuals, the impetus of God's grace converts people, and they become the agents of change in society. But one can read Rauschenbusch and more generally imagine a social view of salvation in a way that reverses the order of its personal and social dimensions. God's general will extends to a society and community that solidaristically takes care of its members. God's grace is not only mediated personally to individuals who then make up a community. Grace also subsists in the relationships that bind people together in healthy life-enhancing exchanges. One cannot really imagine an individual experience without the influences of the communities in which one participates. "Thy kingdom come" refers to a corporate thing in which people participate and are graced and saved because they subsist as a community in relationships that God intends. Grace reaches out through social structures and draws people into its saving relationships. Nothing is lost in this shift, but, once again, it rearranges one's view of things and modifies the basic structure of spirituality. Its appeal reaches out less to personal satisfaction and more as an invitation to participate in a larger movement of being God's agents in the task of social well-being.

A Turn to Jesus of Nazareth

Both Rauschenbusch and Day turned to Jesus of Nazareth as a direct source of inspiration for their spirituality. They did not do so for the same reason; they had their own incentives. Rauschenbusch was stirred when he heard Fr. Edward McGlynn, at a political rally for New York's mayoral election, cite Jesus' prayer: "Thy Kingdom come! Thy will be done on earth."[8] Here was an interpretation of Jesus' teaching that addressed the crisis he was facing in his congregation. Gradually the turn to Jesus, and seeing him from the viewpoint of the rule of God that he preached, released a set of meanings for people living in community rather than shaping each individual life. Jesus spoke to Israel, not only to individuals. The content of Jesus' spirituality took on a new socially relevant meaning and eventually transformed the meaning of what Jesus did for human salvation and the meaning of atonement theory. For the social gospel the rule of God was a metaphor that opened up the gospel for a new appropriation, closer to Jesus' own sensibility to the will of God "on earth."

Dorothy Day, too, turned to Jesus of Nazareth, but she thought more in line with Thomas à Kempis's imitation of Christ. Also, she interpreted Jesus from a radical perspective as noted earlier. "To help the organizers, to give what you have for relief, to pledge yourself to voluntary poverty for life so that you can share with your brothers is not enough. One must live with them, share with them their suffering too. Give up one's privacy, and mental and spiritual comforts as well as physical."[9] Day was thinking in terms of the revelation of the end time in Matthew 25. But it is hard to read these words and not think of her own life. Day's turn to Jesus radicalizes Kant's categorical imperative. But the radicality of Day's social commitment does not ignore the individual because her socialism is grounded in personalism. The social crisis was desperate because of the value of the individual persons who were being destroyed.

But more is going on in this turn to the historical Jesus of Nazareth than the Christocentrism of these spiritualities. The turn to history, to the social suffering and oppression, reflects questioning, a critical spirit, and a quest for points of Christian leverage that go deeper than the doctrinal formulas. This critical spirit differs from what the Bible offered the Reformers in the sixteenth century who for the most part accused people of personal sin. It seeks to penetrate the New Testament narrative and find the inspiration of Jesus himself. This critical spirit knows that Jesus' teaching has to take new forms in the present time. Past doctrines in themselves do not satisfy, because the language of the traditional doctrines and moral teachings do not foster a spirituality that meets the present situation. Without interpretation, appropriation, and methods of application they remain past history. Both Rauschenbusch and Day were bringing traditional doctrine and spirituality into a new situation and proposing new relevant meanings for actual life in a unique social situation.

The Anatomy of Spirituality

The texts of Walter Rauschenbusch and Dorothy Day focus attention on the beginning of the present-day period. They incorporate within themselves the Enlightenment, American experience, and the deeper historical and social consciousness that was generated in the nineteenth century. They communicate forcefully a corporate responsibility for the world in which we live at any given time. They set the stage for spiritual writers after them that reflect issues raised during the last one hundred years that use the language of liberation. But they also raise a new set of questions about the basic structure of spirituality and pointedly Christian life. Their writing and lives revolve around the question of how to communicate a social interpretation of spirituality in a way that can be internalized by individuals. An answer to that question requires an understanding of the anatomy of spirituality itself.

In this series the working definition of spirituality has been "the way persons and groups lead their lives in relation to what they consider ultimate." Concretely, in the discussion of Christian spirituality, the ultimate refers to God as God has been revealed in the Bible with particular focus on Jesus Christ. The many authors considered up to this point have illustrated Christian spirituality across Western history and revealed substantial variation in its historical manifestations. But within the differences one can discern structural or constitutive dimensions of spirituality that remain invariant. Insofar as one can distinguish in human life the functions of knowing, willing, and acting, one can distinguish a parallel set of influences at work in all spiritualities. Does one of these three functions that structure spirituality provide the center of gravity for the other two?

The first is the analogue of knowledge, the set of Christian beliefs that define a specifically Christian vision of things that provides the intelligibility of Christian living and points the way for willing and acting. The second is willing itself, the act of intentional determination and commitment to act in a certain way. In some writers, the center of gravity of all spirituality seems to come down to a basic commitment of moral sensibility generally and certain values in particular. The third dimension of spirituality occupies a prominent place in the working definition itself: spirituality consists of action, the way people lead their lives. The other dimensions do not effectively exist outside of the active living of one's life.

The question of the anatomy of spirituality asks how these three facets of subjectivity relate to each other. Comprehensive spirituality includes faith-knowledge, a pure intention or committed direction of one's life, and action itself. But where is the leading edge? (1) A vision provided by faith provides the framework of life. All act within the imaginary constituted by basic beliefs. Christian beliefs define the very nature of Christian spirituality and guide it by the content of the doctrines. This, and this alone, makes doctrinal theology so important. (2) But consistently, from the New Testament through the desert Fathers and Cassian and thereafter, purity of heart defines the core of spirituality. Value determines commitment: what one considers good defines what one lives for. So much of Christian spirituality revolves around finding and following the will of God. Take the foundational morality out of spirituality and it dies. (3) But just as firmly and consistently Jesus' teaching insists that action is what finally unites a person with God. The key that opens up an actual spirituality does not consist in knowledge or value but in what people do. Action alone makes belief and intention real. Ultimately people define themselves and their relation to God by their actions.

Undoubtedly these three dimensions are all entwined within each other in an integrated spirituality. Normally, knowing spontaneously leads to willing and action. Action must be intentional and not blind. One's basic desire and commitment enlist knowing to sharpen its view and action to prove that the dedication is real. And even if knowing and willing are off key, human actions define the character of persons and constitute their relation to God. The analysis of how these dimensions relate to each other, therefore, provides a deep understanding of Christian spirituality. Determining the "center" or the "keystone" of the arch will provide a template for understanding and comparing the plurality of forms that Christian spirituality takes.

The question of the anatomy of spirituality is of course abstract; it is also difficult to determine that one analysis rules out another because of the complex interaction of the structural dimensions. The formula may differ with individuals, and cultures too might carry different emphases. But analysis provides a context for mediating an expansion of the very idea of spirituality that is needed in our time. It helps to chart the way in which a social spirituality can be communicated to individual persons. People have to be able to understand that social problems are rooted in a corporate subjectivity that is supported by individuals. One has to communicate the power of a social vision and cause. Individuals have to see how their personal activity may be constricted by social bias or expanded by new insight and possibility. Can daily life also be part of a larger positive movement to which they really contribute? Spirituality cannot be understood individualistically today;

individualism almost always suffers from a myopic framework that distorts understanding, valuation, and action. In sum, the social perspective that captured the imagination of Rauschen-busch and Day represents a turning point for understanding Christian spirituality that compares in size to the transitions that occurred in the Reformation and the Enlightenment.

*   *   *   *

Between the premodern history of spirituality and the present time lie the yawning canyon of Enlightenment and the devel-opment of a strong historical and social consciousness. On the far side of this gap, spirituality seemed to be straightfor-ward; one could read Jesus' teachings off the pages of the New Testament, and one could adjust them to the various historical situations in which they were heard. But the radical critique of Christian authority and the relativization of all transcendent faith knowledge to historical and social opinion have weakened the authority of spiritual language and, on the world scene, relegated it to partisan bias. It turned Chris-tian spirituality into private devotion and broke its connection with the common weal.

But this does not correspond with Christian experience; it does not represent the consciousness of Christian faith itself. Christians believe, as do others, that their faith and the beliefs that express it correspond with reality, however difficult it is to verify the transcendent application. Faith is not whistling in the dark; it illumines life. But today one cannot take that correspondence for granted, even when one is talking to oneself. Faith in today's world needs critical appropriation. It cannot be sectarian language proclaimed in a bubble. Spir-itual language spoken within the church has to correlate with wider everyday life. On the public level of society, it has to show its relationship with the social, political, and economic worlds. In this light, Rauschenbusch and Day appear as mark-ers that exhibit ways of addressing this new situation for

Christians' spirituality. Each of them shows in a distinctive way that Christian spirituality must include a dimension of concern for and engagement in life in the world. It cannot be separated from the moral social sphere, any more than the public arena can be divorced from moral exigency. These witnesses open a way of connecting Christian spirituality to the public conversations of our own time.

Notes

1. Sydney Ahlstrom wrote that the social gospel was "a movement which has been widely hailed at home and abroad as the most distinctive contribution of the American churches to world Christianity." *A Religious History of the American People* (New Haven: Yale University Press, 1972), 786.

2. Rauschenbusch, *A Theology for the Social Gospel*, 119–20.

3. The characterization of Day's response to the social crisis as accompaniment should not be taken in a reductionist way. It did not exclude public confrontation and protest. Her commitment transcended accompaniment, recognized social causes for poverty, and addressed negative social structural issues. She explicitly says, "We did not feel that Christ meant we should remain silent in the face of injustice and accept it even though he said, 'The poor ye shall always have with you.'" *The Long Loneliness*, 205.

4. Ibid., 221.

5. Her personalism finds expression frequently in observations such as this description of the people in the houses of hospitality [and those who are fed there]: "They are stripped then, not only of all earthly goods, but of spiritual goods, their sense of human dignity. When they are forced into line at municipal lodging houses, in clinics, in our houses of hospitality, they are then the truly destitute." Ibid., 215.

6. Rauschenbusch is explicit about this. He writes that one of the great reactions against the church's authority resulted in "a system of religious individualism in which the social forces of salvation were slighted, and God and the individual were almost the only realities in sight." *A Theology for the Social Gospel*, 123.

7. Such broad statements cannot be pressed too far. Churches always reacted to and became fiercely engaged when political society threatened their institutional self-interest or attacked the public relevance of their morality. Both Rauschenbusch and Day were aware of individualism and privatism in their respective churches. Rauschenbusch had to proceed with caution and erudition in the face of Baptist leadership, and Day was aware of the charge that "when it came to private morality the Catholics shone but when it came to social and political morality, they were often conscienceless." *The Long Loneliness*, 210.

8. Minus, citing Rauschenbusch, in *Walter Rauschenbusch*, 62.

9. Day, *The Long Loneliness*, 214.

Further Reading

Day, Dorothy. *All the Way to Heaven: The Selected Letters of Dorothy Day*. Edited by Robert Ellsberg. New York: Image Books, 2010. [These letters, beginning in 1923 and ending in 1980, allow Dorothy Day intimately to speak for herself along her way through these tumultuous years in American history.]

———. *Dorothy Day: Selected Writings*. [Originally *By Little and By Little*.] Edited and introduced by Robert Ellsberg. Maryknoll, N.Y.: Orbis Books, 1992. [These selected writings, organized thematically by topic, allow a reader to focus on particular areas that Dorothy Day came back to over her lifetime.]

Evans, Christopher Hodge. *The Kingdom Is Always but Coming: A Life of Walter Rauschenbusch*. Grand Rapids: Eerdmans, 2004. [This biography tells the story of Rauschenbusch's family, his social awakening during the period of his ministry in Hell's Kitchen, and his work to animate the social gospel movement.]

Forest, Jim. *All Is Grace: A Biography of Dorothy Day*. Maryknoll, N.Y.: Orbis Books, 2011. [Forest revises and expands earlier biographies and communicates his intimate personal knowledge of Dorothy Day and the Catholic Worker movement.]

Hudson, Winthrop S., ed. *Walter Rauschenbusch: Selected Writings*. Sources of American Spirituality. New York: Paulist Press, 1984. [This volume underlines the evangelical sources of Rauschenbusch's spirituality that held true across his conversion to the social gospel.]

Loughery, John. *Dorothy Day: Dissenting Voice of the American Century*. New York: Simon & Schuster, 2020. [A full biography of the life of Dorothy Day through her gradual conversion and commitment to a radical life of witness to the values of Catholic faith sometimes over against the church.]

Minus, Paul M. *Walter Rauschenbusch: American Reformer*. New York: Macmillan, 1988. [Paul Minus tells the story of Rauschenbusch's family, formation, and ministry as pastor and professor in a concise and readable way.]

Peitz, Darlene Ann. *Solidarity as Hermeneutic: A Revisionist Reading of the Theology of Walter Rauschenbusch*. New York: Peter Lang, 1992. [This book interprets the deep structure of Rauschenbusch's spirituality through the hermeneutics of reinterpretation of the classic message of Jesus in order to meet the challenges of the social devastation left in the wake of the industrial revolution.]

Smucker, Donovan E. *Origins of Walter Rauschenbusch's Social Ethics*. Montreal: Queens School of Policy Studies, 1994. [After charting the chronology of Rauschenbusch's thought, this work analyzes how pietism, his Baptist roots, social liberalism, and the desire for Christian transformation of society fed into Rauschenbusch's synthesis.]

About the Series

The volumes of this series provide readers direct access to important voices in the history of the faith. Each of the writings has been selected, first, for its value as a historical document that captures the cultural and theological expression of a figure's encounter with God. Second, as "classics," the primary materials witness to the "transcendent" in a way that has proved potent for the formation of Christian life and meaning beyond the particularities of the setting of its authorship.

Recent renewed interest in mysticism and spirituality have encouraged new movements, contributed to a growing body of therapeutic-moral literature, and inspired the recovery of ancient practices from Church tradition. However, the meaning of the notoriously slippery term "spirituality" remains contested. The many authors who write on the topic have different frameworks of reference, divergent criteria of evaluation, and competing senses of the principal sources or witnesses. This situation makes it important to state the operative definition used in this series. *Spirituality is the way people live in relation to what they consider to be ultimate.* So defined, spirituality is a universal phenomenon: everyone has one, whether they can fully articulate it or not. Spirituality emphasizes lived experience and concrete expression of one's principles, attitudes, and convictions, whether rooted in a defined tradition or not. It includes not only interiority and devotional practices but also the real outworkings of people's ideas and values. Students of spirituality examine the way that a person or group conceives of a meaningful existence through the practices that orient them toward their horizon of deepest meaning. What animates their life? What motivates their truest desires? What sustains them and instructs them? What provides for them a vision of the good life? How do they define and pursue truth? And how do they imagine and work to realize their shared vision of a good society?

The "classic" texts and authors presented in these volumes, though they represent the diversity of Christian traditions, define their ultimate value in God through Christ by the Spirit. They share a conviction that the Divine has revealed God's self in history through Jesus Christ. God's self-communication, in turn, invites a response through faith to participate in an intentional life of self-transcendence and to co-labor with the Spirit in manifesting the reign of God. Thus, *Christian spirituality refers to the way that individuals or social entities live out their encounter with God in Jesus Christ by a life in the Spirit.*

Christian spirituality necessarily involves a hermeneutical task. Followers of Christ set about the work of integrating knowledge and determining meaning through an interpretative process that refracts through different lenses: the life of Jesus, the witness of the scripture, the norms of the faith community, the traditions and social structures of one's heritage, the questions of direct experience, the criteria of the academy and other institutions that mediate truthfulness and viability, and personal conscience. These seemingly competing authorities can leave contemporary students of theology with more quandaries than clarity. Thus, this series has anticipated this challenge with an intentional structure that will guide students through their encounter with classic texts. Rather than providing commentary on the writings themselves, this series invites the audience to engage the texts with an informed sense of the context of their authorship and a dialog with the text that begins a conversation about how to make the text meaningful for theology, spirituality, and ethics in the present.

Most of the readers of these texts will be familiar with critical historical methods which enable an understanding of scripture in the context within which it was written. However, many people read scripture according to the common sense understanding of their ordinary language. This almost inevitably leads to some degree of misinterpretation. The Bible's content lies embedded in its cultural context, which is foreign to the experience of contemporary believers. Critical historical study enables a reader to get closer to an authentic past meaning by explicitly attending to the historical period, the situation of the author, and other particularities of the composition of the text. For example, one would miss the point of the story of the "Good Samaritan" if one did not recognize that the first-century Palestinian conflict between Jews and Samaritans makes the hero of the Jewish parable an enemy and an unlikely model of virtue! Something deeper than a simple offer of neighborly love is going on in this text.

However, the more exacting the critical historical method becomes, the greater it increases the distance between the text and the present-day reader. Thus, a second obstacle to interpreting classics for contemporary theology, ethics, and spirituality lies in a bias that texts embedded in a world so different from today cannot carry an inner authority for present life. How can we find something both true and relevant for faith today in a witness that a critical historical method determines to be in some measure alien? The basic problem has two dimensions: how do we appreciate the past witnesses of our tradition on their own terms, and, once we have, how can we learn from something so dissimilar?

Most Christians have some experience navigating this dilemma through biblical interpretation. Through Church membership, Christians have gained familiarity with scriptural language, and preaching consistently applies its content to daily life. But beyond the Bible, a long history of cultural understanding, linguistic innovation, doctrinal negotiations, and shifting patterns of practices has added layer upon layer of meaning to Christian spirituality. Veiled in unfamiliar grammar, images, and politics, these texts may appear as cultural artifacts suitable only for scholarly treatments. How can a modern student of theology understand a text cloaked in an unknown history and still encounter in it a transcendent faith that animates life in the present? Many historical and theological aspects of Christian spirituality that are still operative in communities of faith are losing traction among swathes of the population, especially younger generations. Their premises have been called into question; the metaphors are dead; the symbols appear unable to mediate grace; and the ideas appear untenable. For example, is the human species really saved by the blood of Jesus on the cross? What does it mean to be resurrected from the dead? How does the Spirit unify if the church is so divided? On the other hand, the positive experiences and insights that accrued over time and added depth to Christian spirituality are being lost because they lack critical appropriation for our time. For example, has asceticism been completely lost in present-day spirituality or can we find meaning for it today? Do the mystics live in another universe, or can we find mystical dimensions in religious consciousness today? Does monasticism bear meaning for those who live outside the walls?

This series addresses these questions with a three-fold strategy. The historical first step introduces the reader to individuals who represent key ideas, themes, movements, doctrinal developments, or remarkable distinctions in theology, ethics, or spirituality. This first section will equip readers with a sense of the context of the authorship and a grammar for understanding the text.

Second, the reader will encounter the witnesses in their own words. The selected excerpts from the authors' works have exercised great influence in the history of Christianity.

Letting these texts speak for themselves will enable readers to encounter the wisdom and insight of these classics anew. Equipped with the necessary background and language from the introduction, students of theology will bring the questions and concerns of their world into contact with the world of the authors. This move personalizes the objective historical context and allows the existential character of the classic witness to appear. The goal is not the study of the exact meaning of ancient texts, as important as that is. That would require a task outside the scope of this series. Recommended readings will be provided for those who wish to continue digging into this important part of interpretation. These classic texts are not presented as comprehensive representations of their authors but as statements of basic characteristic ideas that still have bearing on lived experience of faith in the twenty-first century. The emphasis lies on existential depth of meaning rather than adequate representation of an historical period which can be supplemented by other sources.

Finally, each volume also offers a preliminary interpretation of the relevance of the author and text for the present. The methodical interpretations seek to preserve the past historical meanings while also bringing them forward in a way that is relevant to life in a technologically developed and pluralistic secular culture. Each retrieval looks for those aspects that can open realistic possibilities for viable spiritual meaning in current lived experience. In the unfolding wisdom of the many volumes, many distinct aspects of the Christian history of spirituality converge into a fuller, deeper, more far-reaching, and resonant language that shows what in our time has been taken for granted, needs adjustment, or has been lost (or should be). The series begins with fifteen volumes but, like Cassian's *Conferences*, the list may grow.

About the Editors

Roger Haight is a Visiting Professor at Union Theological Seminary in New York. He has written several books in the area of fundamental theology. A graduate of the University of Chicago, he is a past president of the Catholic Theological Society of America.

Alfred Pach III is an Associate Professor of Medical Sciences and Global Health at the Hackensack Meridian School of Medicine. He has a Ph.D. from the University of Wisconsin in Madison and an MDiv in Psychology and Religion from Union Theological Seminary.

Amanda Avila Kaminski is an Assistant Professor of Theology at Texas Lutheran University, where she also serves as Director of the program in Social Innovation and Social Entrepreneurship. She has written extensively in the area of Christian spirituality.

Past Light on Present Life:
Theology, Ethics, and Spirituality

Roger Haight, SJ, Alfred Pach III,
and *Amanda Avila Kaminski,* series editors

Available titles:

Western Monastic Spirituality: John Cassian, Caesarius of Arles,
    and Benedict
On the Medieval Structure of Spirituality: Thomas Aquinas
Grace and Gratitude: Spirituality in Martin Luther
Spirituality of Creation, Evolution, and Work: Catherine Keller
    and Pierre Teilhard de Chardin
Spiritualities of Social Engagement: Walter Rauschenbusch
    and Dorothy Day